THE COMPLETE DIABETIC COOKBOOK FOR BEGINNERS

1500 Days of Healthy and Savory Recipes for Prediabetes, Diabetes, and Type 2 Diabetes Newly Diagnosed. Eat Healthier without Sacrificing the Good Taste.|Full Color Pictures Version|With 30-Day Healthy Meal Plan

DOROTHY G. EBERLY

Copyright© 2022 By Dorothy G. Eberly Rights Reserved

This book is copyright protected. It is only for personal use. You cannot amend, distribute, sell, use, quote or paraphrase any part of the content within this book, without the consent of the author or publisher.

Under no circumstances will any blame or legal responsibility be held against the publisher, or author, for any damages, reparation, or monetary loss due to the information contained within this book, either directly or indirectly.

Disclaimer Notice:

Please note the information contained within this document is for educational and entertainment purposes only. All effort has been executed to present accurate, up to date, reliable, complete information. No warranties of any kind are declared or implied. Readers acknowledge that the author is not engaged in the rendering of legal, financial, medical or professional advice. The content within this book has been derived from various sources. Please consult a licensed professional before attempting any techniques outlined in this book.

By reading this document, the reader agrees that under no circumstances is the author responsible for any losses, direct or indirect, that are incurred as a result of the use of the information contained within this document, including, but not limited to, errors, omissions, or inaccuracies.

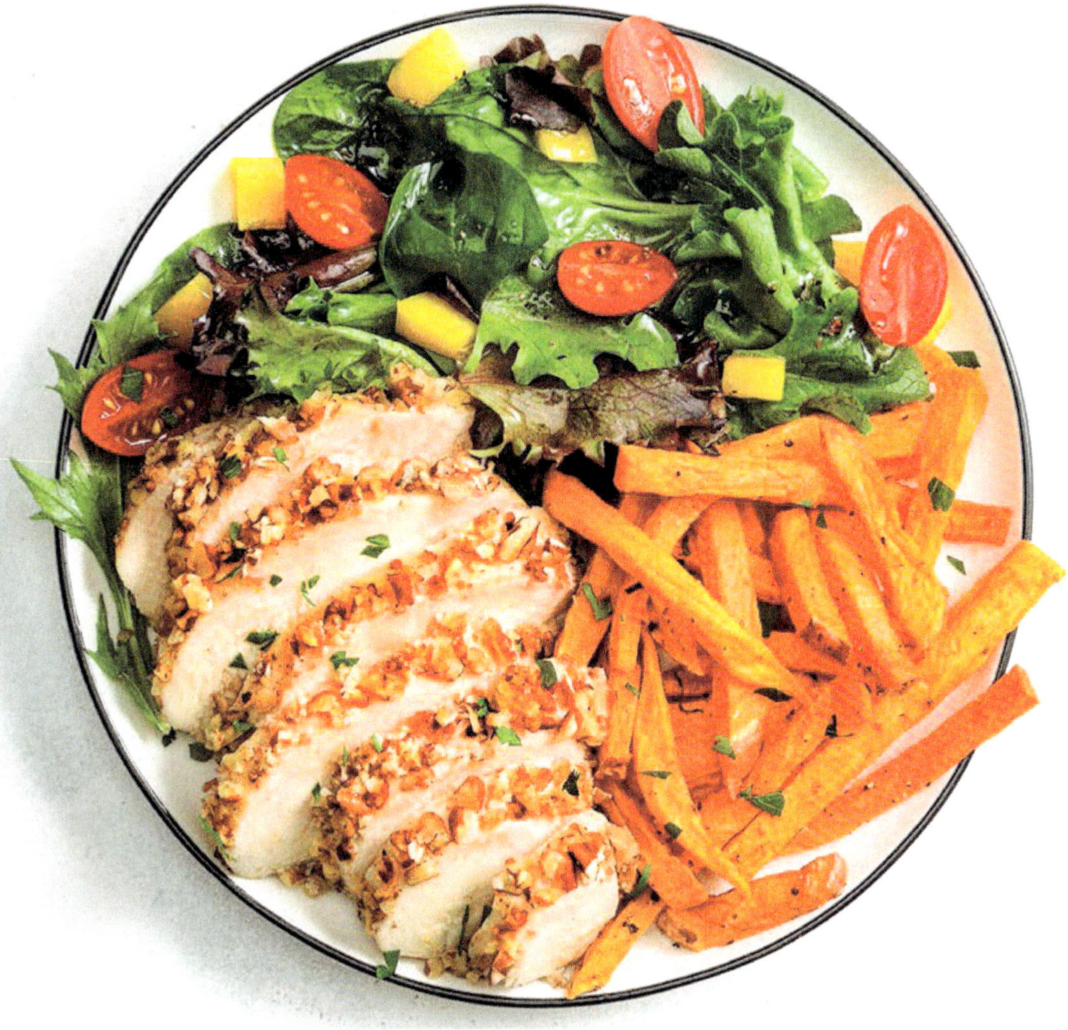

Table of Contents

Introduction 1

Chapter 1
Basics of Diabetic Diet 2
What is Diabetes and the Diabetic Diet? 3
The Importance of the Diabetic Diet 3
The Main Goals and Benefits of a Diabetic Diet 3

Chapter 2
Planning a Diabetic Diet 5
Meal Planning for Diabetics 6
Components of a Balanced Diabetic Diet 6
Portion sizes and controlling calories 7

Chapter 3
Managing Diabetes Through Diet 8
How to Monitor Blood Sugar Levels 9
Special Occasions and Eating Out 9
Developing a Personalized Plan with your Healthcare Provider .. 10

Chapter 4
30 Days Meal Plan 11

Chapter 5
Breakfast 14
Apple Cheddar Muffins 15
Apple Cinnamon Scones 15
Creamy Cheese Stuffed French Toast 16
Apple Filled Swedish Pancake 16
Oat and Walnut Granola 17
Walnut and Oat Granola 17
Avocado Lemon Toast 18
Healthy Cottage Cheese Pancakes 18
Spinach Egg Scramble on Bread 19
Greek Yogurt Sundae 19
Apple Cinnamon Muffins 20
Savory Grits 20
Pineapple-Grapefruit Smoothie 21
Coconut-Berry Sunrise Smoothie 21
Coconut and Berry Smoothie 22
Scallion Grits with Shrimp 22
Huevos Rancheros Remix 22

Chapter 6
Chicken and Poultry 23
Sheet-Pan Chicken Parmesan with Cauliflower 24
Grilled Turkey Tenderloin 24
Garlic with Broiled Chicken 24
Asian Roasted Duck Legs 24
Balsamic Chicken & Vegetable Skillet 25
Shawarma Chicken with Chickpeas and Sweet Potato 25
Chicken Breasts with Carrots & Zucchini Stuffing 25
Spice-Rubbed Crispy Roast Chicken 25
BBQ Chicken & Noodles 26
Cheesy Chicken & "Potato" Casserole 26

Black Beans Chicken Stew	27
Parmesan Topped Chicken	27
Chicken Livers Hawaiian with Bean Sprouts	28
Turkey Stuffed Red Bell Peppers	28
Easy Coconut Chicken Tenders	29
Tuscan-Style Rosemary Chicken	29
Chicken Caesar Salad	30
Creamy and Aromatic Chicken	30
Turkey Kabob with Pitas	31
Goat Cheese Stuffed Chicken Breasts	31
Turkey Burgers	32
Skillet Chicken with Okra and Tomato	32
Cajun Chicken & Pasta	33
Cashew Chicken	33

Chapter 7
Beef, Lamb and Pork — 34

Easy Mu Shu Pork	35
Skillet Pork Loin with Pears	35
Alfredo Sausage & Vegetables	35
Bacon & Cauliflower Casserole	36
Pork Carnitas	36
Pork Chops with Pears & Cabbage	36
Beef & Broccoli Skillet	37
Lamb and Mushroom Cheese Burgers	37
Easy Beef Curry	37
BBQ Pork Tacos	37
Caribbean Bowls	38
Beef & Veggie Quesadillas	38
Asian Beef Bowls	39
Steak with Asparagus	39
Bunless Sloppy Joes	40
Beef Kabobs with Vegetables	40
Easy Rib-Eye Steak	41
Cherry-Glazed Lamb Chops	41
Beef and Zucchini Lasagna	41

Chapter 8
Fish and Seafood — 42

Tomato Tuna Melts	43
Peppercorn-Crusted Baked Salmon	43
Celery Fish Salad	43
Coastal Creole Shrimp	43
Jumpin' Jambalaya	44
Lazy Sushi	44
Roasted Salmon with Honey-Mustard Sauce	44
Shrimp Stir-Fry	45
Low Country Boil	45
Fish Tacos	45
Herbed Fish Fillets	46
Baked Fish	46
Shrimp Scampi	46

Chapter 9
Vegetable and Side Dishes — 47

Tomato Vegetable Soup	48
Chipotle Twice-Baked Sweet Potatoes	48
Broccoli and Squash Medley	48
Herb Seasoned Broccoli	48
Navy Bean Soup with Spinach	49
Zucchini Basil Muffins	49
Molted Vegetable Salad	49
Chili Relleno Casserole	49
Baked Tomatoes	50
Asian Fried Eggplant	50
Butternut Fritters	50
Cauliflower Mushroom Risotto	50

Chapter 10
Soups, Salads, and Sandwiches — 51

Asian Noodle Salad	52
Baked "Potato" Salad	52
Comforting Summer Squash Soup with Crispy Chickpeas	52
Beef and Mushroom Barley Soup	53
Roasted Carrot Leek Soup	53
Red Lentil Soup	53
Lamb Vegetable Stew	54
Thai Peanut and Shrimp Soup with Carrots	54
Tomato and Kale Soup	54
Irish Lamb Stew	54
Classic Gazpacho	55
Gazpacho	55
Avocado and Goat Cheese Toast	55
Harvest Salad	55
Chopped Vegetable-Barley Salad	56
Cauliflower Leek Soup	56
Roasted Tomato Bell Pepper Soup	56
Kale Cobb Salad	56

Chapter 11
Snacks and Desserts — 57

Apple Pie Parfait	58
Roasted Squash with Thyme	58
Grilled Sesame Tofu	58
Parmesan Crisps	58
Jewel Yams with Nutmeg	59
Grilled Peach and Coconut Yogurt Bowls	59
Tomato Mozzarella Skewers	59
Ice Cream with Warm Strawberry Rhubarb Sauce	59
Raspberry Pumpkin Muffin	60
Easy Cauliflower Hush Puppies	60
Garlicky Kale Chips	60
Banana and Carrot Flax Muffins	61
Berry Smoothie Pops	61
Cauliflower Mash	61
Apple Crunch	61

Appendix 1 Measurement Conversion Chart — 62
Appendix 2 The Dirty Dozen and Clean Fifteen — 63
Appendix 3 Index — 64

Introduction

Life of a diabetic patient can be very painful. Tiredness, idleness, and many more are their common problem. The most painful thing is they can not eat whatever they want. Eating carelessly can increase their sugar level and put their lives in danger. No medicine ends diabetics, but it can be controlled with a perfect diet. Many people have a misconception that a diabetic diet is not tasty and always bland. The good news is that is not true, there are many ways you can eat tasty food without any danger. If you are tired of eating bland food and want something exciting on your plate, you have your hands on the right book. For understanding this cookbook better you have to understand what diabetics are and how it works.

Diabetes is a very common disease nowadays. It might not be a deadly disease itself but it can lead to fatal situations. To stay alive, body cells need energy that comes from food. Any food we eat turns into glucose after digestion. The glucose has to enter the cells to utilize the glucose into energy. Here it needs help from a hormone called insulin. Insulin helps glucose to enter the cell walls. This hormone is produced by an organ called the pancreas.

Diabetic is a state where the pancreas can not produce insulin or the production is lesser than body demand. A lack of insulin means lesser glucose is entering the cell. As the cells are not receiving enough glucose it makes them weak and more vulnerable. Extra glucose that could not enter the cell stays in the blood. The unused extra glucose in the body causes many problems and that's what diabetes is. Diabetics can lead to many fatal organ problems like blindness, kidney problems, heart problems, and many more.

To live a healthy life as a diabetic patients have to follow some diet. The diet changes per meal like for breakfast, lunch, and dinner. And different kinds of diabetes require different diets. This cookbook has recipes for every kind of diabetes and they are clinically proven and safe. There are plenty of recipes that are suitable for diabetic patients of any age. Some of the recipes are unique and new, so read them properly for better understanding.

This cookbook is suitable for anyone who can read, the recipes are briefly explained. Even a person who does not have any previous cooking experience can cook like a master chef with this book.

As an author, I must give the right information. Before writing this book, I studied everything related to diabetes. This cookbook is not an ordinary cookbook, it can be a token of love. Gift it to your friends and family who are affected by diabetes. It will help them enjoy their life with better food on their plates.

All the recipes listed in this book are personally tested so you do no need to be worried about them. Try out these healthy recipes and live a healthy and tasty life.

Chapter 1
Basics of Diabetic Diet

What is Diabetes and the Diabetic Diet?

Diabetes is a chronic condition that affects the way the body processes sugar or glucose. People with diabetes either do not produce enough insulin, the hormone that helps to regulate blood sugar levels, or their body does not effectively use the insulin it produces. As a result, their blood sugar levels can become too high, leading to a range of health problems.

Managing diabetes through diet is an important part of controlling blood sugar levels and preventing complications. By following a healthy and balanced diabetic diet, people with diabetes can stabilize their blood sugar levels and support overall good health. A diabetic diet typically includes a variety of fruits, vegetables, whole grains, lean proteins, and healthy fats, and it is carefully balanced with medication and physical activity to ensure that blood sugar levels remain within a healthy range.

The Importance of the Diabetic Diet

The importance of following a healthy and balanced diet when you have diabetes cannot be overstated. A nutritious and well-planned diet is essential for people with diabetes, as it can help to control blood sugar levels, prevent complications, and support overall good health.

When blood sugar levels are not properly controlled, it can lead to a range of health problems, including heart disease, nerve damage, kidney damage, and vision loss. By following a healthy and balanced diabetic diet, people with diabetes can keep their blood sugar levels within a healthy range and reduce their risk of complications.

A healthy and balanced diabetic diet can also provide other benefits, such as weight loss, improved energy levels, and better overall health. By choosing nutrient-dense foods and limiting unhealthy and high-calorie options, people with diabetes can support their physical and emotional well-being and enjoy a better quality of life.

It is time to take an active role in managing your diabetes by making informed and mindful choices about your nutrition.

The Main Goals and Benefits of a Diabetic Diet

Controlling blood sugar levels: A diabetic diet is designed to help people with diabetes keep their blood sugar levels within a healthy range. By balancing their intake of carbohydrates with medication and physical activity, people with diabetes can prevent their blood sugar levels from becoming too high or too low, which can lead to a range of health problems.

Preventing complications: Uncontrolled blood sugar levels can lead to a range of complications, such as heart disease, nerve damage, kidney damage, and vision loss.

Supporting weight loss: A diabetic diet is often lower in calories and unhealthy fats than a typical Western diet, and it can help people with diabetes to lose weight and maintain a healthy body weight. This can have numerous health benefits, including improved blood sugar control, reduced risk of heart disease and other complications, and better overall health.

Improving energy levels: A nutritious and balanced diet can provide the body with the fuel it needs to function properly and maintain energy levels throughout the day. By choosing nutrient-dense foods, people with diabetes can support their physical and mental energy and stay active and healthy.

Supporting overall health and well-being: A healthy and balanced diabetic diet can provide numerous benefits for overall health and well-being. It can provide essential nutrients, fiber, and other beneficial compounds, and it can support healthy digestion, immune function, and mental health. By following a diabetic diet, people with diabetes can enjoy better overall health and a better quality of life.

- Understanding Carbohydrates and Blood Sugar

HOW CARBOHYDRATES AFFECT BLOOD SUGAR LEVELS

Carbohydrates are one of the main types of nutrients that provide the body with energy. They are found in a wide range of foods, including fruits, vegetables, grains, and dairy products. When we eat carbohydrates, they are broken down into glucose, which is the main source of fuel for our cells.

For people with diabetes, carbohydrates can affect blood sugar levels in several ways. First, the body uses insulin to help regulate the amount of glucose in the blood. When we eat carbohydrates, the body produces more insulin, which helps to move glucose from the bloodstream into the cells, where it can be used for energy.

However, if the body does not produce enough insulin or if the body does not effectively use the insulin it produces, blood sugar levels can become too high. This can lead to a range of health problems, such as heart disease, nerve damage, and kidney damage.

In order to manage their blood sugar levels, people with diabetes need to carefully balance their intake of carbohydrates with medication and physical activity. By doing this, they can ensure that their blood sugar levels remain within a healthy range and reduce their risk of complications.

DIFFERENT TYPES OF CARBOHYDRATES

There are three main types of carbohydrates: sugars, starches, and fiber. Each type of carbohydrate has a different effect on blood sugar levels, and it is important for people with diabetes to understand the differences in order to manage their blood sugar effectively.

Sugars are simple carbohydrates that are found naturally in fruits, vegetables, and dairy products, and they are also added to many processed foods and beverages. They are quickly broken down by the body into glucose, which can cause a rapid rise in blood sugar levels. For this reason, people with diabetes should limit their intake of added sugars, and they should choose fruits and other carbohydrate sources that are lower in natural sugars.

Starches are complex carbohydrates that are found in grains, starchy vegetables, and legumes. They take longer to break down into glucose than sugars, so they have a slower and more gradual effect on blood sugar levels. However, they can still affect blood sugar levels, so people with diabetes should be mindful of their intake of starches and balance them with medication and physical activity.

Fiber is a type of carbohydrate that is found in fruits, vegetables, and whole grains. Unlike sugars and starches, fiber is not broken down into glucose, so it does not affect blood sugar levels. In fact, fiber can help to slow the absorption of glucose from other carbohydrate sources, and it can promote healthy digestion and blood sugar control. For this reason, people with diabetes should aim to include plenty of fiber-rich foods in their diet.

BALANCING CARBOHYDRATES WITH MEDICATION AND PHYSICAL ACTIVITY

Balancing carbohydrates with medication and physical activity is an essential part of managing blood sugar levels for people with diabetes. When we eat carbohydrates, our body produces insulin to help regulate the amount of glucose in the blood. However, if the body does not produce enough insulin or if the body does not effectively use the insulin it produces, blood sugar levels can become too high.

For example, if a person with diabetes eats a meal that is high in carbohydrates, they may need to adjust their medication dose or increase their physical activity in order to prevent their blood sugar levels from becoming too high. On the other hand, if a person with diabetes does not eat enough carbohydrates, their blood sugar levels may become too low, which can also be dangerous.

Chapter 2
Planning a Diabetic Diet

Meal Planning for Diabetics

Meal planning is an important part of managing diabetes through diet. By planning their meals in advance, people with diabetes can ensure that they are eating a healthy and balanced diet that meets their nutritional needs and helps to control their blood sugar levels.

MEAL PLANNING CAN HELP PEOPLE WITH DIABETES TO:

Choose nutrient-dense foods that provide essential vitamins, minerals, and other beneficial compounds

Avoid or limit foods that are high in sugar, saturated fat, and calories

Balance their intake of carbohydrates, protein, and fat to support healthy blood sugar control

Monitor their portion sizes and calorie intake to support weight management

Plan for special occasions and eating out, and make healthy choices when dining out

Taking the time to plan their meals in advance allows people with diabetes to make informed and mindful choices

about their nutrition, so they can support their health and well-being.

Components of a Balanced Diabetic Diet

A balanced diabetic diet typically includes the following components:

Fruits: Fruits are a healthy and nutritious choice for people with diabetes. They are a good source of vitamins, minerals, and fiber, and they are naturally low in calories and fat. When choosing fruits, people with diabetes should aim to include a variety of colorful fruits, such as berries, citrus fruits, and stone fruits. They should also limit their intake of fruits that are high in natural sugars, such as bananas, mangos, and grapes.

Vegetables: Vegetables are an essential part of a healthy and balanced diabetic diet. They are a good source of vitamins, minerals, and fiber, and they are naturally low in calories and carbohydrates. When choosing vegetables, people with diabetes should aim to include a variety of colorful and leafy greens, such as spinach, kale, and broccoli. They should also include starchy vegetables, such as sweet potatoes and squash, in moderation.

Whole grains: Whole grains are a healthy and nutritious choice for people with diabetes. They are a good source of fiber, vitamins, and minerals, and they can help to stabilize blood sugar levels. When choosing whole grains, people with diabetes should aim to include whole wheat, brown rice, quinoa, and oats. They should limit their intake of refined grains, such as white bread and pasta, which are lower in fiber and nutrients.

Lean proteins: Lean proteins are an important part of a balanced diabetic diet. They are a good source of essential amino acids, and they can help to stabilize blood sugar levels. When choosing proteins, people with diabetes should aim to include lean meats, such as chicken and turkey, as well as plant-based proteins, such as beans and lentils. They should limit their intake of high-fat proteins, such as bacon and sausage, which are high in saturated fat and calories.

Healthy fats: healthy fats provide essential fatty acids, and they can support heart health and blood sugar control. When choosing healthy fats, people with diabetes should aim to include the following:

Monounsaturated fats: Monounsaturated fats are found in a variety of foods, including nuts, seeds, avocados, and olive oil. They can help to lower bad cholesterol levels, and they can support blood sugar control.

Polyunsaturated fats: Polyunsaturated fats are found in a variety of foods, including fatty fish, walnuts, and vegetable oils. They can help to lower bad cholesterol levels, and they can support healthy blood sugar control.

Omega-3 fatty acids: Omega-3 fatty acids are found in fatty fish, such as salmon, mackerel, and sardines, as well as in plant-based sources, such as flaxseeds and chia seeds. They can help to reduce inflammation, and they can support heart health and blood sugar control.

When choosing healthy fats, people with diabetes should aim to include a variety of monounsaturated, polyunsaturated, and omega-3 fatty acids in their diet. They should also limit their intake of unhealthy fats, such as saturated fats and trans fats, which can increase bad cholesterol levels and increase the risk of heart disease.

Portion sizes and controlling calories

Portion sizes and calorie control are important for weight management for people with diabetes. By managing their portion sizes and calorie intake, people with diabetes can maintain a healthy body weight, which can support blood sugar control and reduce the risk of complications.

When it comes to portion sizes, people with diabetes should aim to eat balanced meals that include a variety of healthy foods in appropriate amounts. They should use measuring cups and food scales to help them gauge the appropriate portion sizes for different foods, and they should be mindful of the serving sizes listed on food labels.

In terms of calorie control, people with diabetes should aim to consume an appropriate number of calories to support their health and well-being. This will depend on factors such as their age, gender, height, weight, and activity levels. By working with a healthcare provider, people with diabetes can determine the appropriate calorie intake for their individual needs, and they can make healthy and balanced food choices that support weight management.

Managing portion sizes and calorie intake is an important part of weight management for people with diabetes. Being mindful of the amount of food they eat and the number of calories they consume helps people with diabetes support their health and well-being, and reduce their risk of complications.

Chapter 3
Managing Diabetes Through Diet

Meal timing and consistency play an important role in managing diabetes. By eating at regular intervals and choosing balanced and nutritious meals, people with diabetes can support their blood sugar control and reduce the risk of complications.

When it comes to meal timing, people with diabetes should aim to eat at regular intervals throughout the day, typically every three to four hours. This can help to prevent blood sugar levels from becoming too high or too low, and it can support healthy energy levels and concentration.

In terms of meal consistency, people with diabetes should aim to eat balanced and nutritious meals at each mealtime. They should include a variety of fruits, vegetables, whole grains, lean proteins, and healthy fats, and they should limit their intake of sugar, saturated fat, and calories. By eating balanced and nutritious meals, people with diabetes can support their blood sugar control and reduce their risk of complications.

Meal timing and consistency are important factors in managing diabetes. By eating at regular intervals and choosing balanced and nutritious meals, people with diabetes can support their health and well-being, and they can reduce their risk of complications.

How to Monitor Blood Sugar Levels

Monitoring blood sugar levels and adjusting medication and diet accordingly is an important part of managing diabetes. By regularly checking their blood sugar levels, people with diabetes can gain a better understanding of how their diet, medication, and physical activity affect their blood sugar levels, and they can make informed and mindful choices to support healthy blood sugar control.

There are several ways that people with diabetes can monitor their blood sugar levels, including:

Blood glucose meter: A blood glucose meter is a small device that uses a drop of blood to measure the amount of glucose in the blood. People with diabetes can use a blood glucose meter at home or on the go to check their blood sugar levels.

Continuous glucose monitor (CGM): A continuous glucose monitor (CGM) is a small device that is worn on the skin. It uses a sensor to measure the glucose levels in the fluid under the skin, and it provides real-time glucose readings throughout the day and night.

Glycated hemoglobin (A1C) test: A glycated hemoglobin (A1C) test is a blood test that measures the average blood sugar levels over the past two to three months. It is typically done in a healthcare provider's office, and it can provide a broad overview of a person's blood sugar control over time.

Once people with diabetes have checked their blood sugar levels, they can adjust their medication and diet accordingly. If their blood sugar levels are too high, they may need to adjust their medication dose or increase their physical activity. If their blood sugar levels are too low, they may need to eat more carbohydrates or adjust their medication dose.

Special Occasions and Eating Out

Special occasions and eating out can be challenging for people with diabetes, but with some planning and mindfulness, it is possible to enjoy these occasions while still following a healthy and balanced diabetic diet.

Here are some tips for handling special occasions and eating out while following a diabetic diet:

Plan ahead: Before attending a special occasion or dining out, people with diabetes should take the time to plan their meals. They can look at the menu in advance, and they can choose dishes that are lower in sugar, saturated fat, and calories. They can also plan to bring their own snacks or share a dish with a friend or family member in order to avoid overindulging.

Choose wisely: When attending a special occasion or dining out, people with diabetes should make mindful choices about the foods they eat. They can choose dishes that are rich in vegetables, lean proteins, and healthy fats, and they can limit their intake of processed foods, fried foods, and desserts. They can also ask for sauces and dressings on the side, and they can request that their food be cooked without added sugar or unhealthy fats.

Portion control: On special occasions and when dining out, people with diabetes should be mindful of their portion sizes. They can use measuring cups and food scales to help them gauge the appropriate portion sizes for different foods, and they can avoid overserving themselves. They can also use smaller plates and bowls, and they can eat slowly and mindfully in order to avoid overeating.

Handling special occasions and eating out while following a diabetic diet requires some planning and mindfulness, but through making informed and mindful choices, people with diabetes can still enjoy special occasions and dining out.

Developing a Personalized Plan with your Healthcare Provider

If you have diabetes, it is important to work with a healthcare provider to develop a personalized plan for managing your condition through diet. A healthcare provider can provide you with expert guidance and support, and they can help you to create a diet plan that meets your individual needs and goals.

Here are some reasons why working with a healthcare provider is beneficial for managing diabetes through diet:

Expert guidance: A healthcare provider can provide you with expert guidance and support for managing your diabetes through diet. They can help you to understand the role of carbohydrates, proteins, and fats in your diet, and they can provide you with practical tips and strategies for making healthy and balanced food choices.

Personalized plan: A healthcare provider can help you to develop a personalized plan for managing your diabetes through diet. They can take into account your individual needs, goals, and preferences, and they can create a diet plan that is tailored to your specific situation.

Ongoing support: A healthcare provider can provide you with ongoing support and guidance for managing your diabetes through diet. They can monitor your progress, and they can provide you with advice and support as needed. They can also adjust your diet plan as needed in response to changes in your health or lifestyle.

Overall, working with a healthcare provider is an important step for managing diabetes through diet. By seeking expert guidance and support, you can create a personalized plan for managing your diabetes, and you can achieve your health goals and support your well-being.

Chapter 4
30 Days Meal Plan

Days	Breakfast	Lunch	Dinner
Day 1	Apple Cinnamon Scones	Grilled Turkey Tenderloin	Tomato Tuna Melts
Day 2	Apple Filled Swedish Pancake	Tomato Vegetable Soup	Skillet Pork Loin with Pears
Day 3	Oat and Walnut Granola	Navy Bean Soup with Spinach	Chili Relleno Casserole
Day 4	Creamy Cheese Stuffed French Toast	Garlic with Broiled Chicken	Butternut Fritters
Day 5	Spinach Egg Scramble on Bread	Baked Tomatoes	Lazy Sushi
Day 6	Apple Cheddar Muffins	Asian Noodle Salad	Roasted Carrot Leek Soup
Day 7	Greek Yogurt Sundae	Pork Carnitas	Molted Vegetable Salad
Day 8	Healthy Cottage Cheese Pancakes	Asian Fried Eggplant	Black Beans Chicken Stew
Day 9	Apple Cinnamon Muffins	Zucchini Basil Muffins	Grilled Turkey Tenderloin
Day 10	Walnut and Oat Granola	Celery Fish Salad	Baked "Potato" Salad
Day 11	Pineapple-Grapefruit Smoothie	Tomato and Kale Soup	Beef & Broccoli Skillet
Day 12	Avocado Lemon Toast	Irish Lamb Stew	Asian Beef Bowls
Day 13	Savory Grits	Gazpacho	Roasted Tomato Bell Pepper Soup
Day 14	Coconut-Berry Sunrise Smoothie	Caribbean Bowls	Asian Beef Bowls
Day 15	Apple Cheddar Muffins	Broccoli and Squash Medley	Shrimp Stir-Fry
Day 16	Pineapple-Grapefruit Smoothie	Asian Beef Bowls	Fish Tacos
Day 17	Coconut and Berry Smoothie	Easy Mu Shu Pork	Bunless Sloppy Joes
Day 18	Huevos Rancheros Remix	Lamb Vegetable Stew	Asian Roasted Duck Legs

Day 19	Savory Grits	Asian Beef Bowls	Avocado and Goat Cheese Toast
Day 20	Scallion Grits with Shrimp	Classic Gazpacho	Bunless Sloppy Joes
Day 21	Apple Cinnamon Scones	Garlic with Broiled Chicken	Red Lentil Soup
Day 22	Oat and Walnut Granola	Herb Seasoned Broccoli	Coastal Creole Shrimp
Day 23	Oat and Walnut Granola	Easy Beef Curry	Easy Rib-Eye Steak
Day 24	Savory Grits	Celery Fish Salad	Easy Mu Shu Pork
Day 25	Walnut and Oat Granola	Coastal Creole Shrimp	Cauliflower Leek Soup
Day 26	Walnut and Oat Granola	Low Country Boil	Coastal Creole Shrimp
Day 27	Apple Cheddar Muffins	Harvest Salad	BBQ Pork Tacos
Day 28	Oat and Walnut Granola	Celery Fish Salad	Irish Lamb Stew
Day 29	Creamy Cheese Stuffed French Toast	BBQ Chicken & Noodles	Easy Rib-Eye Steak
Day 30	Savory Grits	Asian Beef Bowls	Cauliflower Mushroom Risotto

The Complete Diabetic Cookbook for Beginners | 13

Chapter 5
Breakfast

Apple Cheddar Muffins
Prep time: 10 minutes | Cook time: 20 minutes | Serves 12

- 1 egg
- ¾ cup tart apple, peel & chop
- 2/3 cup reduced fat cheddar cheese, grated
- 2/3 cup skim milk
- 2 cup low carb baking mix
- 2 tbsp. vegetable oil
- 1 tsp cinnamon.

1. Heat oven to 400 degrees F. Line a 12 cup muffin pan with paper liners.
2. In a medium bowl, lightly beat the egg. Stir in remaining Ingredients just until moistened. Divide evenly between prepared muffin cups.
3. Bake 17-20 minutes or until golden brown. Serve warm.

PER SERVING

Calories: 162 | Total Carbohydrates: 17g | Net Carbohydrates: 13g | Protein: 10g | Fat: 5g | Suger: 8g | Fiber: 4g

Apple Cinnamon Scones
Prep time: 5 minutes | Cook time: 25 minutes | Serves 16

- 2 large eggs
- 1 apple, diced
- ¼ cup + ½ tbsp. margarine, melted and divided
- 1 tbsp. half-n-half
- 3 cups almond flour
- 1/3 cup + 2 tsp Splenda
- 2 tsp baking powder
- 2 tsp cinnamon
- 1 tsp vanilla
- ¼ tsp salt

1. Heat oven to 325 degrees. Line a large baking sheet with parchment paper.
2. In a large bowl, whisk flour, 1/3 cup Splenda, baking powder, 1 ½ teaspoons cinnamon, and salt together. Stir in apple.
3. Add the eggs, ¼ cup melted margarine, cream, and vanilla. Stir until the mixture forms a soft dough.
4. Divide the dough in half and pat into 2 circles, about 1-inch thick, and 7-8 inches around.
5. In a small bowl, stir together remaining 2 teaspoons Splenda, and ½ teaspoon cinnamon.
6. Brush the ½ tablespoon melted margarine over dough and sprinkle with cinnamon mixture. Cut each into 8 equal pieces and place on prepared baking sheet.
7. Bake 20-25 minutes, or until golden brown and firm to the touch.

PER SERVING

Calories: 176 | Total Carbohydrates: 12g | Net Carbohydrates: 9g | Protein: 5g | Fat: 12g | Suger: 8g | Fiber: 3g

Creamy Cheese Stuffed French Toast

Prep time: 5 minutes | Cook time: 20 minutes | Serves 4

- Nonstick cooking spray
- 8 1-inch slices of French bread
- 2 egg whites
- 1 egg, slightly beaten
- 3/4 cup of fat-free milk
- 1/2 cup of fat-free cream cheese (about 5 ounces)
- 2 tablespoons of strawberry or apricot spreadable fruit
- 1/2 teaspoon of vanilla
- 1/8 teaspoon of apple pie spice
- 1/2 cup of strawberry or apricot spreadable fruit

1. Combine cream cheese and 2 tablespoons of spreadable fruit in a small bowl. Form pocks, with a knife, in each of the bread slices.
2. Fill each of the pockets with 1 tablespoon of the cream cheese mixture.
3. Combine the egg whites, vanilla, milk, egg, and apple pie spice in a small bowl.
4. Coat nonstick skillet lightly using cooking spray; heat over medium heat.
5. Dip the stuffed bread slices into the egg mixture (coating each side).
6. Place the bread slices on a hot grill and cook until golden brown for about 3 minutes, turning once.
7. Meanwhile, heat about 1/2 cup of spreadable fruit in a small saucepan until melted, frequently stirring.
8. Serve over french toast, and enjoy!

PER SERVING

Calories: 150 | Fat: 1g | Protein: 7g | Sodium: 163mg | Carbohydrates: 29g

Apple Filled Swedish Pancake

Prep time: 25 minutes | Cook time: 20 minutes | Serves 6

- 2 apples, cored and sliced thin
- ¾ cup egg substitute
- ½ cup fat-free milk
- ½ cup sugar-free caramel sauce
- 1 tbsp. reduced calorie margarine
- ½ cup flour
- 1`1/2 tbsp. brown sugar substitute
- 2 tsp water
- ¼ tsp cinnamon
- 1/8 tsp cloves
- 1/8 tsp salt
- Nonstick cooking spray

1. Heat oven to 400 degrees. Place margarine in cast iron, or ovenproof, skillet and place in oven until margarine is melted.
2. In a medium bowl, whisk together flour, milk, egg substitute, cinnamon, cloves and salt until smooth.
3. Pour batter in hot skillet and bake 20 – 25 minutes until puffed and golden brown.
4. Spray a medium saucepan with cooking spray. Heat over medium heat.
5. Add apples, brown sugar and water. Cook, stirring occasionally, until apples are tender and golden brown, about 4 – 6 minutes.
6. Pour the caramel sauce into a microwave-proof measuring glass and heat 30 – 45 seconds, or until warmed through.
7. To serve, spoon apples into pancake and drizzle with caramel. Cut into wedges.

PER SERVING

Calories: 193 | Total Carbohydrates: 25g | Net Carbohydrates: 23g | Protein: 6g | Fat: 2g | Suger: 12g | Fiber: 2g

Oat and Walnut Granola

Prep time: 10 minutes | Cook time: 30 minutes | Serves 16

- 4 cups rolled oats
- 1 cup walnut pieces
- ½ cup pepitas
- ¼ teaspoon salt
- 1 teaspoon ground cinnamon
- 1 teaspoon ground ginger
- ½ cup coconut oil, melted
- ½ cup unsweetened applesauce
- 1 teaspoon vanilla extract
- ½ cup dried cherries

1. Preheat the oven to 350°F. Line a baking sheet with parchment paper.
2. In a large bowl, toss the oats, walnuts, pepitas, salt, cinnamon, and ginger.
3. In a large measuring cup, combine the coconut oil, applesauce, and vanilla. Pour over the dry mixture and mix well.
4. Transfer the mixture to the prepared baking sheet. Cook for 30 minutes, stirring about halfway through. Remove from the oven and let the granola sit undisturbed until completely cool. Break the granola into pieces, and stir in the dried cherries.
5. Transfer to an airtight container, and store at room temperature for up to 2 weeks.

PER SERVING

Calories: 224 | Total Fat: 15g | Protein: 5g | Carbohydrates: 20g | Sugars: 5g | Fiber: 3g | Sodium: 30mg

Walnut and Oat Granola

Prep time: 10 minutes | Cook time: 30 minutes | Serves 16

- 4 cups rolled oats
- 1 cup walnut pieces
- ½ cup pepitas
- ¼ teaspoon salt
- 1 teaspoon ground cinnamon
- 1 teaspoon ground ginger
- ½ cup coconut oil, melted
- ½ cup unsweetened applesauce
- 1 teaspoon vanilla extract
- ½ cup dried cherries

1. Preheat the oven to 350°F (180°C). Line a baking sheet with parchment paper.
2. In a large bowl, toss the oats, walnuts, pepitas, salt, cinnamon, and ginger.
3. In a large measuring cup, combine the coconut oil, applesauce, and vanilla. Pour over the dry mixture and mix well.
4. Transfer the mixture to the prepared baking sheet. Cook for 30 minutes, stirring about halfway through. Remove from the oven and let the granola sit undisturbed until completely cool. Break the granola into pieces, and stir in the dried cherries.
5. Transfer to an airtight container, and store at room temperature for up to 2 weeks.

PER SERVING

Calories: 225 | Fat: 14.9g | Protein: 4.9g | Carbohydrates: 20.1g | Fiber: 3.1g | Sugar: 4.9g | Sodium: 31mg

Avocado Lemon Toast

Cook time: 13 minutes | Serves 1

- 2 slices Whole-grain bread
- 1/2 Avocado
- 2 tablespoons Fresh cilantro (chopped)
- 1 teaspoon Fresh lemon juice
- ¼ teaspoon Lemon zest
- 1 pinch Cayenne pepper
- 1 pinch Fine sea salt
- ¼ teaspoon Chia seeds

1. Start by taking a medium-sized mixing bowl and adding in the avocado. Use a fork to mash it nicely.
2. Add in the cilantro, lemon zest, lemon juice, sea salt, and cayenne pepper. Mix well until combined.
3. Toast the bread slices in a toaster until golden brown. This should take about 3 minutes.
4. Top the toasted bread slices with the avocado mixture and finish by sprinkling with chia seeds.

PER SERVING

Calories: 72 | Fat: 1.2g | Protein: 3.6g | Carbohydrates: 11.6g

Healthy Cottage Cheese Pancakes

Cook time: 15 minutes | Serves 2

- ½ cup Cottage cheese (low-fat)
- ¼ cup Oats
- ⅓ cup (approx. 2 egg whites) Egg whites
- 1 teaspoon Vanilla extract
- 1 tablespoon Stevia (raw)
- Olive oil cooking spray
- Berries or sugar-free jam (optional)

1. Start by taking a food blender and adding in the egg whites and cottage cheese. Also add in the vanilla extract, a little bit of stevia, and oats. Pulse until the consistency is smooth.
2. Take a nonstick pan and grease it nicely with the cooking spray. Place the pan on a medium flame.
3. Once heated, scoop out half of the batter and pour it on the pan. Cook for about 2½ minutes on each side.
4. Place the cooked pancakes on a serving plate and top with sugar-free jam or berries.

PER SERVING

Calories: 410 | Fat: 1.5g | Protein: 24.5g | Carbohydrates: 19g

Spinach Egg Scramble on Bread
Prep time: 10 minutes | Cook time: 5 minutes | Serves 1

- 1 teaspoon canola oil
- 1½ cups baby spinach
- 2 eggs, lightly beaten
- 1 pinch kosher salt
- 1 pinch black pepper
- 1 slice whole-grain bread
- ½ cup raspberries

1. Inside the small nonstick skillet, add the oil over moderate-high heat.
2. minutes Place the spinach on a serving platter.
3. Clean your pan, set over moderate heat, and crack the eggs into it.
4. Cook, stirring once or twice to ensure equal cooking, for 1-2 minutes, or till just set. Add spinach, salt, and Black pepper, to taste.
5. With toast and strawberries, serve your scramble.

PER SERVING

Calories: 298 | Total Carbohydrates: 20.8g | Net Carbohydrates: 2g | Protein: 17.9g | Fat: 15.9g | Suger: 3g | Fiber: 6g

Greek Yogurt Sundae
Prep time: 5 minutes | Serves 1

- ¾ cup plain nonfat Greek yogurt
- ¼ cup mixed berries (blueberries, strawberries, blackberries)
- 2 tablespoons cashew, walnut, or almond pieces
- 1 tablespoon ground flaxseed
- 2 fresh mint leaves, shredded

1. Spoon the yogurt into a small bowl. Top with the berries, nuts, and flaxseed.
2. Garnish with the mint and serve.

PER SERVING

Calories: 237 | Total Fat: 11g | Protein: 21g | Carbohydrates: 16g | Fiber: 4g | Sugar: 9g | Sodium: 64mg

Apple Cinnamon Muffins

Prep time: 15 minutes | Cook time: 25 minutes | Serves 12

- 1 cup apple, diced fine
- 2/3 cup skim milk
- ¼ cup reduced-calorie margarine, melted
- 1 egg, lightly beaten
- 1 2/3 cups flour
- 1 tbsp. Stevia
- 2 ½ tsp baking powder
- 1 tsp cinnamon
- ½ tsp sea salt
- ¼ tsp nutmeg
- Nonstick cooking spray

1. Heat oven to 400 degrees F. Spray a 12-cup muffin pan with cooking spray.
2. In a large bowl, combine dry Ingredients and stir to mix.
3. In another bowl, beat milk, margarine, and egg to combine.
4. Pour wet Ingredients into dry Ingredients and stir just until moistened. Gently fold in apples.
5. Spoon into prepared muffin pan. Bake 25 minutes, or until tops are lightly browned.

PER SERVING

Calories: 119 | Total Carbohydrates: 17g | Net Carbohydrates: 16g | Protein: 3g | Fat: 4g | Suger: 3g | Fiber: 1g

Savory Grits

Prep time: 5 minutes | Cook time: 7 minutes | Serves 4

- ¼ cup each
- 2 cups water
- 1 cup fat-free milk
- 1 cup stone-ground corn grits

1. In a heavy-bottomed pot, bring the water and milk to a simmer over medium heat.
2. Gradually add the grits, stirring continuously.
3. Reduce the heat to low, cover, and cook, stirring often, for 5 to 7 minutes, or until the grits are soft and tender. Serve and enjoy.

PER SERVING

Calories: 166 | Total Fat: 1g | Cholesterol: 1mg | Sodium: 32mg | Total Carbohydrates: 34g | Sugar: 3g | Fiber: 1g | Protein: 6g

Pineapple-Grapefruit Smoothie

Prep time: 10 minutes | Cook time: 5 minutes | Serves 2

- 1 cup part-skim coconut water
- 1 cup baby spinach
- 1 cup diced pineapple
- 1 grapefruit, peeled and segmented small
- ½ teaspoon ginger, grated
- 1 cup ice

1. Inside the blender, mix the coconut water, ginger, spinach, grapefruit and any juices, pineapple, and ice.
2. Puree till the mixture is smooth and foamy.

PER SERVING

Calories: 102 | Total Carbohydrates: 25.8g | Net Carbohydrates: 2g | Protein: 2g | Fat: 0.9g | Suger: 6g | Fiber: 3g

Coconut-Berry Sunrise Smoothie

Prep time: 5 minutes | Serves 2

- ½ cup mixed berries (blueberries, strawberries, blackberries)
- 1 tablespoon ground flaxseed
- 2 tablespoons unsweetened coconut flakes
- ½ cup unsweetened plain coconut milk
- ½ cup leafy greens (kale, spinach)
- ¼ cup unsweetened vanilla nonfat yogurt
- ½ cup ice

1. In a blender jar, combine the berries, flaxseed, coconut flakes, coconut milk, greens, yogurt, and ice.
2. Process until smooth. Serve.

PER SERVING

Calories: 181 | Total Fat: 15g | Protein: 6g | Carbohydrates: 8g | Fiber: 4g | Sugar: 3g | Sodium: 24mg

Coconut and Berry Smoothie

Prep time: 5 minutes | Cook time: 0 minutes | Serves 2

- ½ cup mixed berries (blueberries, strawberries, blackberries)
- 1 tablespoon ground flaxseed
- 2 tablespoons unsweetened coconut flakes
- ½ cup unsweetened plain coconut milk
- ½ cup leafy greens (kale, spinach)
- ¼ cup unsweetened vanilla nonfat yogurt
- ½ cup ice

1. In a blender jar, combine the berries, flaxseed, coconut flakes, coconut milk, greens, yogurt, and ice.
2. Process until smooth.
3. Serve.

PER SERVING

Calories: 182 | Fat: 14.9g | Protein: 5.9g | Carbohydrates: 8.1g | Fiber: 4.1g | Sugar: 2.9g | Sodium: 25mg

Scallion Grits with Shrimp

Prep time: 15 minutes | Cook time: 20 minutes | Serves 6-8

- ¼ cup grits and 4 to 5 shrimp each
- 1½ cups fat-free milk
- 1½ cups water
- 2 bay leaves
- 1 cup stone-ground corn grits
- 2 garlic cloves, minced
- 2 scallions, white and green parts, thinly sliced
- 1 pound medium shrimp, shelled and deveined
- ½ teaspoon dried dill
- ½ teaspoon smoked paprika
- ¼ teaspoon celery seeds

1. In a medium stockpot, combine the milk, water, and bay leaves and bring to a boil over high heat.
2. Gradually add the grits, stirring continuously.
3. Reduce the heat to low, cover, and cook for 5 to 7 minutes, stirring often, or until the grits are soft and tender. Remove from the heat and discard the bay leaves.
4. In a small cast iron skillet, bring the broth to a simmer over medium heat.
5. Add the garlic and scallions, and sauté for 3 to 5 minutes, or until softened.
6. Add the shrimp, dill, paprika, and celery seeds and cook for about 7 minutes, or until the shrimp is light pink but not overcooked.
7. Plate each dish with ¼ cup of grits, topped with shrimp.

PER SERVING

Calories: 197 | Total Fat: 1g | Cholesterol: 149mg | Sodium: 203mg | Total Carbohydrates: 25g | Sugar: 3g | Fiber: 1g | Protein: 20g

Huevos Rancheros Remix

Prep time: 5 minutes | Cook time: 10 minutes | Serves 4

- 1 cup low-sodium black beans, drained and rinsed
- Avocado oil cooking spray
- ½ cup jarred salsa verde
- 8 large eggs
- 1 cup packaged or fresh Pico de Gallo (see here)
- 4 lime wedges

1. Pour the black beans and salsa verde into a small saucepan over low heat and cover. Cook until the beans are heated through, about 10 minutes.
2. Meanwhile, heat a small skillet over medium-low heat. When hot, coat the cooking surface with cooking spray, and fry or scramble the eggs to your liking.
3. For each portion, top 2 eggs with one-quarter of the black beans and pico de gallo. Finish each portion with a squeeze of lime.

PER SERVING

Calories: 210 | Total Fat: 9.4g | Protein: 15g | Carbohydrates: 18g | Fiber: 5g | Sugar: 4g | Sodium: 439mg

Chapter 6
Chicken and Poultry

Sheet-Pan Chicken Parmesan with Cauliflower

Prep time: 10 minutes | Cook time: 20 minutes | Serves 4

- 1 cauliflower head, cut into small florets
- 1 tablespoon olive oil
- Sea salt
- Freshly ground black pepper
- 4 (4-ounce) boneless, skinless chicken breasts, pounded to ½-inch thick
- 2 tomatoes, sliced
- ½ cup grated Parmesan cheese
- 1 tablespoon chopped fresh basil

1. Preheat the oven to 400°F. Line a baking sheet with parchment paper.
2. In a medium bowl, toss the cauliflower and oil until well coated and season with salt and pepper. Spread the cauliflower on half the baking sheet.
3. Lightly season the chicken breasts with salt and pepper.
4. Place the chicken on the empty side of the baking sheet and top each with the tomato slices and Parmesan cheese.
5. Bake for about 20 minutes, or until the chicken is just cooked through and the vegetables are tender.
6. Serve topped with basil.

PER SERVING

Calories: 287 | Total Fat: 10g | Saturated Fat: 3g | Sodium: 383mg | Carbohydrates: 16g | Sugar: 6g | Fiber: 5g | Protein: 33g

---

Grilled Turkey Tenderloin

Prep time: 5 minutes | Cook time: 20 minutes | Serves 4

- 1/4 cup of low-sodium soy sauce
- 1/4 cup of sherry wine or apple juice
- 1/8 teaspoon of black pepper
- 2 tablespoons of crushed onion
- 1 pound of uncooked turkey tenderloin, 3/4 to 1 inches thick
- 1/4 cup of peanut oil
- 2 tablespoons of lemon juice
- 1/8 teaspoon of garlic salt
- 1/4 teaspoon of ground ginger

1. In a shallow pan, blend all marinade ingredients together.
2. Add turkey, turning to coat both sides.
3. Cover; marinate in refrigerator several hours or overnight, turning occasionally.
4. Grill the tenderloins over hot coals, 8-10 mins per side, depending on the thickness.
5. Tenderloins are done when there is no pink in the center - do not overcook.
6. Serve in 1/4 inches thick slices in toasted buns.

PER SERVING

Calories: 154.6 | Fat: 3g | Saturated Fat: 0.5g | Sodium: 321.7mg | Carbohydrates: 1.4g | Sugars: 0.7g | Protein: 28.6g

---

Garlic with Broiled Chicken

Prep time: 15 minutes | Cook time: 30 minutes | Serves 4

- 2 1/2 pounds chicken, quartered
- 6 cloves garlic
- 3/4 teaspoon of powdered rosemary
- Salt & pepper to taste
- Chicken bouillon

1. Rub chicken with 2 crushed garlic cloves and rosemary. Also, add pepper and salt.
2. Allow resting 30 minutes.
3. Place chicken in grill pan and coat top with bouillon.
4. Add a little broth to the pan.
5. Bake, turning when half is done.
6. Coat top sides with broth and 2 more garlic cloves. Baste with leftovers from cooking. Serve and enjoy!

PER SERVING

Calories: 344.3 | Protein: 27.5g | Carbohydrates: 7.7g | Sugar: 6.1g | Fat: 22.4g | Saturated Fat: 3.7g

---

Asian Roasted Duck Legs

Prep time: 10 minutes | Cook time: 90 minutes | Serves 4

- 4 duck legs
- 3 plum tomatoes, diced
- 1 red chili, deseeded and sliced
- ½ small Savoy cabbage, quartered
- 2 tsp fresh ginger, grated
- 3 cloves garlic, sliced
- 2 tbsp. soy sauce
- 2 tbsp. honey
- 1 tsp five-spice powder

1. Heat oven to 350 degrees.
2. Place the duck in a large skillet over low heat and cook until brown on all sides and most of the fat is rendered, about 10 minutes. Transfer duck to a deep baking dish. Drain off all but 2 tablespoons of the fat.
3. Add ginger, garlic, and chili to the skillet and cook 2 minutes until soft. Add soy sauce, tomatoes and 2 tablespoons water and bring to a boil.
4. Rub the duck with the five spice seasoning. Pour the sauce over the duck and drizzle with the honey. Cover with foil and bake 1 hour. Add the cabbage for the last 10 minutes.

PER SERVING

Calories: 211 | Total Carbohydrates: 19g | Net Carbohydrates: 16g | Protein: 25g | Fat: 5g | Suger: 14g | Fiber: 3g

Balsamic Chicken & Vegetable Skillet
Prep time: 10 minutes | Cook time: 20 minutes | Serves 4

- 1 lb. chicken breasts, cut in 1-inch cubes
- 1 cup cherry tomatoes, halved
- 1 cup broccoli florets
- 1 cup baby Bella mushrooms, sliced
- 1 tbsp. fresh basil, diced
- 1/2 recipe homemade pasta, cooked and drain well (chapter 14)
- ½ cup low sodium chicken broth
- 3 tbsp. balsamic vinegar
- 2 tbsp. olive oil, divided
- 1 tsp pepper
- ½ tsp garlic powder
- ½ tsp salt
- ½ tsp red pepper flakes

1. Heat oil in a large, deep skillet over med-high heat. Add chicken and cook until browned on all sides, 8-10 minutes.
2. Add vegetables, basil, broth, and seasonings. Cover, reduce heat to medium and cook 5 minutes, or vegetables are tender.
3. Uncover and stir in cooked pasta and vinegar. Cook until heated through, 3-4 minutes. Serve.

PER SERVING

Calories: 386 | Total Carbohydrates: 11g | Net Carbohydrates: 8g | Protein: 43g | Fat: 18g | Suger: 5g | Fiber: 3g

Shawarma Chicken with Chickpeas and Sweet Potato
Prep time: 10 minutes | Cook time: 20 minutes | Serves 4

- 1 (15-ounce) can low-sodium chickpeas, drained and rinsed
- 1 sweet potato, peeled and cut into ½-inch chunks
- 1 tablespoon olive oil
- 4 teaspoons store-bought shawarma spice, divided
- 1 pound boneless, skinless chicken breast, cut into 1-inch chunks

1. Preheat the oven to 400°F. Line a baking sheet with parchment paper.
2. In a medium bowl, toss the chickpeas, sweet potato, oil, and 1 teaspoon shawarma spice until well combined. Spread the mixture on half of the baking sheet.
3. Add the chicken breast to the bowl and toss with the remaining 3 teaspoons of shawarma spice. Spread the chicken chunks on the other half of the baking sheet.
4. Bake for about 20 minutes, tossing halfway through, until the chicken is cooked through. Serve.

PER SERVING

Calories: 260 | Total Fat: 7g | Saturated Fat: 1g | Sodium: 235mg | Carbohydrates: 20g | Sugar: 4g | Fiber: 5g | Protein: 30g

Chicken Breasts with Carrots & Zucchini Stuffing
Prep time: 15 minutes | Cook time: 40 minutes | Serves 4

- 2 small (whole) skinless, boneless chicken breasts
- 1 cup of carrots, shredded (about 2 small)
- 1 cup of zucchini, shredded (about 1 med.)
- 1 teaspoon of salt
- 1/4 teaspoon of poultry seasoning
- 1 envelope chicken-flavored bouillon
- 1/4 cup of water

1. In a bowl, combine zucchini, carrots, salt, and poultry seasoning.
2. Add about 1/2 cup mixture to each pocket (each breast should open similar to a butterfly); secure with toothpicks.
3. In place chicken in a medium-size skillet, sprinkle with bouillon.
4. Add water to skillet and cook over medium-high heat, heat to boiling.
5. Reduce heat to low; cover and simmer about 40 mins or until chicken is fork tender.
6. Remove toothpicks.
7. Serve and enjoy!

PER SERVING

Calories: 534.9 | Protein: 54.6g | Carbohydrates: 14.3g | Dietary Fiber: 1.6g | Sugar: 2.9g | Fat: 28g | Saturated Fat: 12.9g | Cholesterol: 214.7mg

Spice-Rubbed Crispy Roast Chicken
Prep time: 10 minutes | Cook time: 35 minutes | Serves 6

- 1 teaspoon ground paprika
- 1 teaspoon garlic powder
- ½ teaspoon ground coriander
- ½ teaspoon ground cumin
- ½ teaspoon salt
- ¼ teaspoon ground cayenne pepper
- 6 chicken legs
- 1 teaspoon extra-virgin olive oil

1. Preheat the oven to 400°F.
2. In a small bowl, combine the paprika, garlic powder, coriander, cumin, salt, and cayenne pepper. Rub the chicken legs all over with the spices.
3. In an ovenproof skillet, heat the oil over medium heat. Sear the chicken for 8 to 10 minutes on each side until the skin browns and becomes crisp.
4. Transfer the skillet to the oven and continue to cook for 10 to 15 minutes until the chicken is cooked through and its juices run clear.

PER SERVING

Calories: 276 | Total Fat: 16g | Protein: 30g | Carbohydrates: 1g | Fiber: 0g | Sugar: 0g | Sodium: 256mg

BBQ Chicken & Noodles

Prep time: 10 minutes | Cook time: 25 minutes | Serves 4

- 4 slices bacon, diced
- 1 chicken breast, boneless, skinless, cut into 1-inch pieces
- 1 onion, diced
- 1 cup low fat cheddar cheese, grated
- ½ cup skim milk
- 14 ½ oz. can tomatoes, diced
- 2 cup low sodium chicken broth
- ¼ cup barbecue sauce, (chapter 16)
- 2 cloves garlic, diced fine
- ¼ tsp red pepper flakes
- Homemade noodles, (chapter 15)
- Salt and pepper, to taste

1. Place a large pot over med-high heat. Add bacon and cook until crispy. Drain fat, reserving 1 tablespoon.
2. Stir in chicken and cook until browned on all sides, 3-5 minutes.
3. Add garlic and onion and cook, stirring often, until onions are translucent, 3-4 minutes.
4. Stir in broth, tomatoes, milk, and seasonings. Bring to boil, cover, reduce heat and simmer 10 minutes.
5. Stir in barbecue sauce, noodle, and cheese and cook until noodles are done and cheese has melted, 2-3 minutes. Serve.

PER SERVING

Calories: 331 | Total Carbohydrates: 18g | Net Carbohydrates: 15g | Protein: 34g | Fat: 13g | Suger: 10g | Fiber: 3g

Cheesy Chicken & "Potato" Casserole

Prep time: 10 minutes | Cook time: 40 minutes | Serves 6

- 4 slices bacon, cooked and crumbled
- 3 cups cauliflower
- 3 cups chicken, cooked and chopped
- 3 cups broccoli florets
- 2 cups reduced fat cheddar cheese, grated
- 1 cup fat free sour cream
- 4 tbsp. margarine, soft
- 1 tsp salt
- ½ tsp black pepper
- ½ tsp garlic powder
- ½ tsp paprika
- Nonstick cooking spray

1. In a large saucepan add 4-5 cups of water and bring to a boil. Add the cauliflower and cook about 4-5 minutes, or until it is tender drain well. Repeat with broccoli.
2. Heat oven to 350 degrees. Spray a baking dish with cooking spray.
3. In a medium bowl, mash the cauliflower with the margarine, sour cream and seasonings. Add remaining Ingredients, saving ½ the cheese, and mix well.
4. Spread mixture in prepared baking dish and sprinkle remaining cheese on top. Bake 20-25 minutes, or until heated through and cheese has melted. Serve.

PER SERVING

Calories: 346 | Total Carbohydrates: 10g | Net Carbohydrates: 8g | Protein: 28g | Fat: 15g | Suger: 4g | Fiber: 2g

Black Beans Chicken Stew

Prep time: 10 minutes | Cook time: 30 minutes | Serves 4

- 1 tablespoon vegetable oil
- 4 boneless chicken breast halves
- 1 (10 oz.) can tomatoes with chile peppers, diced
- 1 (15 oz.) can black beans, rinsed
- 1 (8.75 oz.) can kernel corn, drained
- 1 pinch ground cumin

1. In a suitable skillet, heat oil over medium-high heat.
2. Brown chicken breasts on both sides. Add tomatoes with green chile peppers, beans and corn. Reduce heat and let simmer for almost 25 to 30 minutes or until chicken is cooked through and juices run clear.
3. Add a dash of cumin and serve.

PER SERVING

Calories: 310 | Total Carbohydrates: 28g | Net Carbohydrates: 2g | Protein: 35g | Fat: 6g | Suger: 6g | Fiber: 3g

Parmesan Topped Chicken

Prep time: 10 minutes | Cook time: 30 minutes | Serves 4

- 2 tablespoons olive oil
- 1 garlic clove, minced
- 1 cup dry bread crumbs
- ½ cup grated parmesan cheese, non-fat
- 1 teaspoon dried basil leaves
- ¼ teaspoon black pepper
- 6 skinless, boneless chicken breast halves

1. At 350 degrees F, preheat your oven.
2. Lightly grease a 9x13 inch baking pan.
3. In a suitable bowl, blend the garlic with olive oil. In another bowl, toss bread crumbs with parmesan cheese, basil, and pepper.
4. Coat each chicken breast in the oil mixture, then coat with the bread crumb mixture.
5. Place the coated chicken breasts in the prepared baking dish, and top with any remaining bread crumb mixture.
6. Bake 30 minutes in the preheated oven, or until chicken is no longer pink and juices run clear.

PER SERVING

Calories: 281 | Total Carbohydrates: 14g | Net Carbohydrates: 2g | Protein: 30g | Fat: 11g | Suger: 6g | Fiber: 3g

Chicken Livers Hawaiian with Bean Sprouts

Prep time: 10 minutes | Cook time: 10 minutes | Serves 4

- 1/4 cup of liquid chicken bouillon
- 1/2 cup of chopped celery
- 1/2 cup of chopped onion
- 1/2 med. green pepper, sliced
- 12 ounces of chicken livers
- 1 cup of pineapple chunks
- 1 1/4 teaspoon of brown sugar substitute
- 1 teaspoon of salt
- 1 tablespoon of cider vinegar
- Bean sprouts

1. Cook celery, onion, and green pepper in Pam sprayed skillet.
2. Cook over medium-high heat until crisp, for about 5 mins.
3. Add chicken liver and cook 10 mins.
4. Add chicken liver and cook 10 mins.
5. Stir frequently. Add pineapple.
6. Dissolve salt, sugar, and vinegar with 1/2 cup of water. Add to skillet.
7. Serve on cooked hot bean sprouts.

PER SERVING

Calories: 104 | Total Fat: 7g | Saturated Fat: 6g | Sodium: 511mg | Carbohydrates: 8g | Sugar: 5g | Fiber: 2g | Protein: 5g

Turkey Stuffed Red Bell Peppers

Prep time: 15 minutes | Cook time: 50 minutes | Serves 4

- 1 teaspoon extra-virgin olive oil, plus more for greasing the baking dish
- 1 pound (454 g) ground turkey breast
- ½ sweet onion, chopped
- 1 teaspoon minced garlic
- 1 tomato, diced
- ½ teaspoon chopped fresh basil
- Sea salt and freshly ground black pepper, to taste
- 4 red bell peppers, tops cut off, seeded
- 2 ounces (57 g) low-sodium feta cheese

1. Preheat the oven to 350°F (180°C). Lightly grease a baking dish with olive oil and set it aside.
2. Place a large skillet over medium heat and add 1 teaspoon of olive oil. Add the turkey to the skillet and cook until it is no longer pink, stirring occasionally to break up the meat and brown it evenly, about 6 minutes.
3. Add the onion and garlic and sauté until softened and translucent, about 3 minutes. Stir in the tomato and basil. Season with salt and pepper. Place the peppers cut-side up in the baking dish. Divide the filling into four equal portions and spoon it into the peppers. Sprinkle the feta cheese on top of the filling.
4. Add ¼ cup of water to the dish and cover with aluminum foil. Bake the peppers until they are soft and heated through, about 40 minutes.

PER SERVING

Calories: 282 | Fat: 14.1g | Protein: 24.1g | Carbohydrates: 14g | Fiber: 4.1g | Sugar: 9g | Sodium: 270mg

Easy Coconut Chicken Tenders

Prep time: 10 minutes | Cook time: 20 minutes | Serves 6

- 4 chicken breasts, each cut lengthwise into 3 strips
- ½ teaspoon salt
- ¼ teaspoon freshly ground black pepper
- ½ cup coconut flour
- 2 eggs, beaten
- 2 tablespoons unsweetened plain almond milk
- 1 cup unsweetened coconut flakes

1. Preheat the oven to 400°F. Line a baking sheet with parchment paper.
2. Season the chicken pieces with the salt and pepper.
3. Place the coconut flour in a small bowl. In another bowl, mix the eggs with the almond milk. Spread the coconut flakes on a plate.
4. One by one, roll the chicken pieces in the flour, then dip the floured chicken in the egg mixture and shake off any excess. Roll in the coconut flakes and transfer to the prepared baking sheet.
5. Bake for 15 to 20 minutes, flipping once halfway through, until cooked through and browned.

PER SERVING
Calories: 216 | Total Fat: 13g | Protein: 20g | Carbohydrates: 9g | Fiber: 6g | Sugar: 2g | Sodium: 346mg

Tuscan-Style Rosemary Chicken

Cook time: 30 minutes | Serves 1

- 3 tablespoons Butter
- 1½ tablespoons Olive oil
- 3 cloves Garlic
- 3 large Chicken breasts (boneless and skinless)
- ½ cup Red wine vinegar
- 1 teaspoon Salt
- 1 cup Dry vermouth
- 3 tablespoons Fresh rosemary
- ¾ teaspoon Pink peppercorns

1. Start by cutting all 3 chicken breasts in half. Use a kitchen paper towel to blot any excess water from the chicken breasts.
2. Take a large nonstick skillet and place it on a medium-high flame. Add in the olive oil and butter.
3. Once the butter is melted, toss in the garlic cloves and let them cook for around 30 seconds. Remove the garlic cloves from the oil and discard.
4. Place the chicken breasts in the skillet and cook for 2 minutes. Flip over and cook for another 2 minutes.
5. Reduce the flame to medium. Pour the vinegar into the skillet and sprinkle with salt. Cover with a lid and cook the chicken breasts for another 5 minutes.
6. Now toss in the vermouth and rosemary. Let the chicken cook without the lid for around 10 minutes.
7. Transfer the chicken breasts to a platter and let the juices remain in the pan.
8. Add the peppercorns to the remaining juices in the pan and let the sauce boil for around 5 minutes. Make sure the sauce is slightly thickened.
9. Pour the prepared sauce over the chicken breasts and serve hot!

PER SERVING
Fat: 11.4g | Protein: 16.6g | Carbohydrates: 0.9g

Chicken Caesar Salad

Prep time: 10 minutes | Cook time: 15 minutes | Serves 2

- 1 garlic clove
- ½ teaspoon anchovy paste
- Juice of ½ lemon
- 2 tablespoons extra-virgin olive oil
- 1 (8-ounce) boneless, skinless chicken breast
- ¼ teaspoon salt
- Freshly ground black pepper
- 2 romaine lettuce hearts, cored and chopped
- 1 red bell pepper, seeded and cut into thin strips
- ¼ cup grated Parmesan cheese

1. Preheat the broiler to high.
2. In a blender jar, combine the garlic, anchovy paste, lemon juice, and olive oil. Process until smooth and set aside.
3. Cut the chicken breast lengthwise into two even cutlets of similar thickness. Season the chicken with the salt and pepper, and place on a baking sheet.
4. Broil the chicken for 5 to 7 minutes on each side until cooked through and browned. Cut into thin strips.
5. In a medium mixing bowl, toss the lettuce, bell pepper, and cheese. Add the dressing and toss to coat. Divide the salad between 2 plates and top with the chicken.

PER SERVING

Calories: 292 | Total Fat: 18g | Protein: 28g | Carbohydrates: 6g | Fiber: 2g | Sugar: 3g | Sodium: 706mg

Creamy and Aromatic Chicken

Prep time: 15 minutes | Cook time: 30 minutes | Serves 4

- 4 (4-ounce) boneless chicken breasts
- Salt and black pepper, to taste
- 1 tablespoon olive oil
- ½ sweet onion, chopped
- 2 teaspoons chopped thyme
- 1 cup chicken broth
- ¼ cup heavy whipping cream
- 1 scallion, white and green parts, chopped

1. At 375 degrees F, preheat your oven. Rub the chicken liberally with salt and pepper. Heat the olive oil in an oven-safe skillet over medium-high heat until shimmering. Put the chicken in the skillet and cook for almost 10 minutes or until well browned. Flip halfway through. Transfer onto a platter and set aside.
2. Toss in the onion to the same skillet and sauté for 3 minutes or until translucent. Add the thyme and broth and simmer for 6 minutes or until the liquid reduces in half. Mix in the cream, then put the chicken back to the skillet. Arrange the skillet in the oven and bake for 10 minutes almost. Remove the skillet from the oven and serve them with scallion. Garnish the chicken with black olives, sliced cherry tomatoes, or parsley for more flavor.

PER SERVING

Calories: 287 | Fat: 14g | Net Carbohydrates: 2g | Protein: 34g | Total Carbohydrates: 4g | Suger: 1g | Fiber: 1g

Turkey Kabob with Pitas

Prep time: 25 minutes | Cook time: 15 minutes | Serves 4

- 1 teaspoon whole cumin seeds, crushed
- 1 cup shredded cucumber
- ⅓ cup Roma tomato, chopped
- ¼ cup slivered red onion
- ¼ cup shredded radishes
- ¼ cup snipped cilantro
- ¼ teaspoon black pepper
- 1 pound turkey breast, julienned
- ¼ cup plain Greek yogurt
- 4 whole wheat pita bread rounds (6-inch)

1. Toast the cumin seeds for 1 minute and transfer them to a suitable bowl.
2. Add shredded cucumber, Roma tomato, slivered red onion, radishes, cilantro, and black pepper to the bowl. Mix well.
3. To make the curry blend, combine ½ teaspoon olive oil, 1 teaspoon curry powder, ½ teaspoon ground turmeric, ½ teaspoon ground cumin, ½ teaspoon ground coriander, ¼ teaspoon ground ginger, ⅛ teaspoon of salt, and cayenne pepper.
4. In another bowl, combine curry blend and turkey. Stir to coat.
5. Thread turkey onto skewers. Grill kabobs, uncovered for 6 to 8 minutes or until turkey is no longer pink. Turning kabobs occasionally. Remove turkey from skewers.
6. Spread Greek yogurt on pita bread. Spoon cucumber mixture over yogurt. Top with grilled turkey. Serve.

PER SERVING

Calories: 343 | Total Carbohydrates: 40g | Net Carbohydrates: 5g | Protein: 35g | Fat: 6g | Suger: 6g | Fiber: 3g

Goat Cheese Stuffed Chicken Breasts

Prep time: 15 minutes | Cook time: 30 minutes | Serves 4

- 1 cup chopped roasted red pepper
- 2 ounces (57 g) goat cheese
- 4 Kalamata olives, pitted, finely chopped
- 1 tablespoon chopped fresh basil
- 4 (5-ounce / 142-g) boneless, skinless chicken breasts
- 1 tablespoon extra-virgin olive oil

1. Preheat the oven to 400°F (205°C).
2. In a small bowl, stir together the red pepper, goat cheese, olives, and basil until well mixed.
3. Place the filling in the refrigerator for about 15 minutes to firm it up.
4. Cut a slit horizontally in each chicken breast to create a pocket in the middle.
5. Evenly divide the filling between the chicken breast pockets and secure them closed with wooden toothpicks.
6. Place a large skillet over medium-high heat and add the olive oil.
7. Brown the chicken breasts on both sides, about 10 minutes in total.
8. Transfer to the oven. Bake the chicken breasts until the chicken is cooked through, about 20 minutes.
9. Let the chicken breasts rest for 10 minutes, remove the toothpicks, and serve.

PER SERVING

Calories: 246 | Fat: 9.1g | Protein: 35.1g | Carbohydrates: 3g | Fiber: 1.1g | Sugar: 2g | Sodium: 280mg

Turkey Burgers

Prep time: 10 minutes | Cook time: 20 minutes | Serves 4

- 1½ pounds (680 g) lean ground turkey
- ½ cup bread crumbs
- ½ sweet onion, chopped
- 1 carrot, peeled, grated
- 1 teaspoon minced garlic
- 1 teaspoon chopped fresh thyme
- Sea salt and freshly ground black pepper, to taste
- Nonstick cooking spray

1. In a large bowl, mix together the turkey, bread crumbs, onion, carrot, garlic, and thyme until very well mixed.
2. Season the mixture lightly with salt and pepper.
3. Shape the turkey mixture into 4 equal patties.
4. Place a large skillet over medium-high heat and coat it lightly with cooking spray.
5. Cook the turkey patties until golden and completely cooked through, about 10 minutes per side.
6. Serve the burgers plain or with your favorite toppings on a whole-wheat bun.

PER SERVING

Calories: 320 | Fat: 15.1g | Protein: 32.1g | Carbohydrates: 11.9g | Fiber: 1.1g | Sugar: 2g | Sodium: 271mg

Skillet Chicken with Okra and Tomato

Prep time: 15 minutes | Cook time: 25 minutes | Serves 4

- 1 thigh and a heaping spoonful of tomato and okra each
- 4 medium boneless, skinless chicken thighs
- ½ lime
- 1 cup Chicken Broth (here) or store-bought low-sodium chicken broth, divided
- 1 small yellow onion, chopped
- 1 green bell pepper, chopped
- 1 celery stalk, chopped
- 2 garlic cloves, minced
- 8 ounces okra, cut into 1-inch-thick slices
- 4 medium tomatoes, chopped
- 1 tablespoon Creole Seasoning

1. Put the chicken thighs in a small bowl, and squeeze the lime over them.
2. In a large cast iron pan, bring ½ cup of broth to a simmer over medium heat.
3. Add the onion, bell pepper, celery, and garlic and cook, stirring often, for about 5 minutes, or until translucent.
4. Add the okra and a drizzle of broth and cook for 3 minutes, or until the okra is softened.
5. Add the tomatoes and cook for 3 minutes, or until the tomatoes are very soft.
6. Add the chicken, seasoning, and remaining broth.
7. Reduce the heat to low, cover, and cook for 5 to 10 minutes, or until the flavors are married and the chicken is lightly browned.
8. Serve with Savory Skillet Corn Bread.

PER SERVING

Calories: 201 | Total Fat: 5g | Cholesterol: 95mg | Sodium: 133mg | Total Carbohydrates: 15g | Sugar: 6g | Fiber: 4g | Protein: 25g

Cajun Chicken & Pasta

Prep time: 15 minutes | Cook time: 20 minutes | Serves 4

- 3 chicken breasts, boneless, skinless, cut in 1-inch pieces
- 4 Roma tomatoes, diced
- 1 green bell pepper, sliced
- 1 red bell pepper, sliced
- ½ red onion, sliced
- 1 cup half-n-half
- 2 tbsp. margarine
- ¼ cup fresh parsley, diced
- ½ recipe homemade pasta, (chapter 14), cook and drain
- 2 cup low sodium chicken broth
- ½ cups white wine
- 2 tbsp. olive oil
- 3 tsp Cajun spice mix
- 3 cloves garlic, diced fine
- Cayenne pepper, to taste
- Freshly ground black pepper, to taste
- Salt, to taste

1. Place chicken in a bowl and sprinkle with 1 ½ teaspoons Cajun spice, toss to coat.
2. Heat 1 tablespoon oil and 1 tablespoon margarine in a large cast iron skillet over high heat. add chicken, cooking in 2 batches, cook until brown on one side, about 1 minute, flip and brown the other side. Transfer to a plate with a slotted spoon.
3. Add remaining oil and margarine to the pan. Add peppers, onion, and garlic. Sprinkle remaining Cajun spice over vegetables and salt to taste. Cook, stirring occasionally, until vegetables start to turn black, 3-5 minutes. Add tomatoes and cook another 30 seconds. Transfer vegetables to a bowl with a slotted spoon.
4. Add wine and broth to the pan and cook, stirring to scrape up brown bits from the bottom, 3-5 minutes. Reduce heat to med-low and add half-n-half, stirring constantly. Cook until sauce starts to thicken. Taste and season with cayenne, pepper and salt, it should be spicy.
5. Add chicken and vegetables to the sauce and cook 1-2 minutes until hot. Stir in pasta and parsley and serve.

PER SERVING

Calories: 475 | Total Carbohydrates: 21g | Net Carbohydrates: 17g | Protein: 38g | Fat: 25g | Suger: 10g | Fiber: 4g

Cashew Chicken

Prep time: 10 minutes | Cook time: 10 minutes | Serves 4

- 1 lb. skinless boneless chicken breast, cut in cubes
- 1/2 onion, sliced
- 2 tbsp. green onion, diced
- ½ tsp fresh ginger, peeled and grated
- 1 cup whole blanched cashews, toasted
- 1 clove garlic, diced fine
- 4 tbsp. oil
- 2 tbsp. dark soy sauce
- 2 tbsp. hoisin sauce
- 2 tbsp. water
- 2 tsp cornstarch
- 2 tsp dry sherry
- 1 tsp Splenda
- 1 tsp sesame seed oil

1. Place chicken in a large bowl and add cornstarch, sherry, and ginger. Stir until well mixed.
2. In a small bowl, whisk together soy sauce, hoisin, Splenda, and water stirring until smooth.
3. Heat the oil in a wok or a large skillet over high heat. Add garlic and onion and cook, stirring until garlic sizzles, about 30 seconds.
4. Stir in chicken and cook, stirring frequently, until chicken is almost done, about 2 minutes.
5. Reduce heat to medium and stir in sauce mixture. Continue cooking and stirring until everything is blended together. Add cashews and cook 30 seconds.
6. Drizzle with sesame oil, and cook another 30 seconds, stirring constantly. Serve immediately garnished with green onions.

PER SERVING

Calories: 483 | Total Carbohydrates: 19g | Net Carbohydrates: 17g | Protein: 33g | Fat: 32g | Suger: 6g | Fiber: 2g

Chapter 7
Beef, Lamb and Pork

Easy Mu Shu Pork

Prep time: 15 minutes | Cook time: 15 minutes | Serves 4

- 1 tablespoon olive oil
- 1 pound boneless pork loin chops, thinly sliced
- 4 cups sliced fresh white mushrooms
- 2 teaspoons minced garlic
- ½ small cabbage head, finely shredded
- 2 tablespoons low-sodium soy sauce
- 1 tablespoon rice vinegar
- 1 teaspoon toasted sesame oil
- ⅛ teaspoon red pepper flakes
- 8 (6-inch) whole-wheat tortillas
- 1 scallion, both white and green parts, thinly sliced on a bias
- 2 tablespoons sesame seeds

1. In a large skillet, heat the olive oil over medium-high heat and sauté the pork for about 6 minutes, until it is just cooked through. Using a slotted spoon, transfer the pork to a plate and set it aside.
2. Add the mushrooms and garlic and sauté for about 5 minutes, until softened and slightly caramelized. Add the cabbage and bell pepper and sauté for about 4 minutes, until tender-crisp.
3. Add the pork back to the skillet along with the soy sauce, rice vinegar, sesame oil, and red pepper flakes. Toss to combine and serve scooped into the tortillas and topped with scallions and sesame seeds.

PER SERVING

Calories: 398 | Total Fat: 14g | Saturated Fat: 4g | Sodium: 504mg | Carbohydrates: 38g | Sugar: 6g | Fiber: 10g | Protein: 34g

Skillet Pork Loin with Pears

Prep time: 10 minutes | Cook time: 18 minutes | Serves 4

- 1 pound boneless pork loin, thinly sliced
- Sea salt
- Freshly ground black pepper
- 1 tablespoon olive oil
- 3 large pears, cored and cut into 1-inch chunks
- ½ sweet onion, chopped
- 1 teaspoon peeled and grated fresh ginger
- ¼ cup unsweetened apple juice
- 1 teaspoon chopped fresh thyme

1. Season the pork lightly with salt and pepper.
2. In a large skillet, heat the oil over medium-high heat. Sauté the pork for about 6 minutes, until it is browned and just cooked through. Using a slotted spoon, transfer the pork to a plate and set it aside.
3. Add the pears, onion, and ginger and sauté for about 7 minutes, until lightly caramelized. Add the pork back to the skillet along with the apple juice and thyme and simmer for 5 minutes.
4. Serve with your favorite cooked grains or a mixed green salad.

PER SERVING

Calories: 301 | Total Fat: 8g | Saturated Fat: 2g | Sodium: 100mg | Carbohydrates: 31g | Sugar: 18g | Fiber: 7g | Protein: 26g

Alfredo Sausage & Vegetables

Prep time: 10 minutes | Cook time: 15 minutes | Serves 6

- 1 pkg. smoked sausage, cut in ¼-inch slices
- 1 cup half-and-half
- ½ cup zucchini, cut in matchsticks
- ½ cup carrots, cut in matchsticks
- ½ cup red bell pepper, cut in matchsticks
- ½ cup peas, frozen
- ¼ cup margarine
- ¼ cup onion, diced
- 2 tbsp. fresh parsley, diced
- ½ recipe Homemade Pasta, cook & drain, (chapter 15)
- 1/3 cup reduced fat parmesan cheese
- 1 clove garlic, diced fine
- Salt & pepper, to taste

1. Melt margarine in a large skillet over medium heat. Add onion and garlic and cook, stirring occasionally, 3-4 minutes or until onion is soft.
2. Increase heat to med-high. Add sausage, zucchini, carrots, and red pepper. Cook, stirring frequently, 5-6 minutes, or until carrots are tender crisp.
3. Stir in peas and half-n-half, cook 1-2 minutes until heated through. Stir in cheese, parsley, salt, and pepper. Add pasta nd toss to mix. Serve.

PER SERVING

Calories: 283 | Total Carbohydrates: 18g | Net Carbohydrates: 14g | Protein: 21g | Fat: 15g | Suger: 8g | Fiber: 4g

Bacon & Cauliflower Casserole

Prep time: 15 minutes | Cook time: 20 minutes | Serves 6

- 6 slices bacon, cooked and crumbled, divided
- 3 scallions, sliced thin, divided
- 5 cup cauliflower
- 2 cup cheddar cheese, grated and divided
- 1 cup fat free sour cream
- ½ tsp salt
- ¼ tsp fresh cracked pepper
- Nonstick cooking spray

1. Heat oven to 350 degrees. Spray casserole dish with cooking spray.
2. Steam cauliflower until just tender.
3. In a large bowl, combine cauliflower, sour cream, half the bacon, half the scallions and half the cheese. Stir in salt and pepper. Place in prepared baking dish and sprinkle remaining cheese over top.
4. Bake 18-20 minutes until heated through. Sprinkle remaining scallions and bacon over top and serve.

PER SERVING

Calories: 332 | Total Carbohydrates: 15g | Net Carbohydrates: 11g | Protein: 21g | Fat: 20g | Suger: 6g | Fiber: 4g

Pork Carnitas

Prep time: 15 minutes | Cook time: 0 minutes | Serves 6

- 2 teaspoons of finely shredded lime peel
- 2 tablespoons of lime juice
- 12 (16 inches) crisp corn tortillas
- 2 scallions, thinly sliced
- 1/3 cup of light dairy sour cream (Optional)
- 1/3 cup of purchased salsa (Optional)
- 1 (2 pounds) boneless pork shoulder roast, cut into 2-inch pieces
- 1/4 teaspoon of salt
- 1/4 teaspoon of ground pepper
- 1 tablespoon of whole black peppercorns
- 2 teaspoons of cumin seeds
- 4 cloves garlic, minced
- 1 teaspoon of dried oregano, crushed
- 3 bay leaves
- 2 (14 ounces) cans of reduced-sodium chicken broth

1. Sprinkle pork with salt & pepper—place in a 3 1/2- or 4-quart slow cooker.
2. To make a bouquet garni, cut a 6-inch square from a double thickness of cheesecloth.
3. Place the garlic, peppercorns, cumin seeds, oregano, and bay leaves in the center of the cheesecloth square.
4. Pull up the corners of the cheesecloth and tie it with kitchen twine. Add to the pot over low heat. Add the broth.
5. Cover and cook on low for 10-12 hours or on High for 4-5 hours.
6. Remove meat from the pot.
7. Discard the bouquet and cooking liquid.
8. Using two forks, coarsely shred the meat. Discard fat.
9. Sprinkle meat with lime juice and lime zest. Toss to mix.
10. Serve over tortillas. Top with scallions and, if not cooked, sour cream and salsa. Enjoy!

PER SERVING

Calories: 318 | Protein: 32g | Carbohydrates: 24g | Dietary Fiber: 4g | Sugar: 1g | Fat: 10g

Pork Chops with Pears & Cabbage

Prep time: 35 minutes | Cook time: 0 minutes | Serves 6

- 1/8 teaspoon of ground black pepper
- 2 teaspoons of canola oil
- 6 cups of coarsely shredded red cabbage
- 1 cup of sliced onion
- 2 medium pears, cored and sliced
- 1/4 cup of cider vinegar
- 2 tablespoons of packed brown sugar
- 1/4 teaspoon of dried sage, crushed
- 6 small pork loin chops, cut 1/2 inch thick (about 2 pounds total)
- 1/2 teaspoon of dried thyme, crushed
- 1/4 teaspoon of salt
- 1/4 teaspoon of dried sage, crushed
- 1 tablespoon of Snipped fresh sage and/or thyme

1. In a small bowl, combine cider vinegar, brown sugar, & 1/4 teaspoon sage.
2. Reserve 1 tablespoon of the mixture. Set both combinations aside.
3. Trim fat from pork chops. Sprinkle pork with the dried thyme, salt, 1/4 teaspoon sage, and pepper.
4. In a very large skillet, heat the oil over medium-high heat. Add pork chops. Cook for about 6 to 8 mins or until pork is slightly pink in the center and juices run clear, turning pork chops once halfway through cooking and brushing with the 1 tablespoon vinegar mixture for the last 1 minute of cooking time. Remove pork chops from skillet. Cover & keep warm.
5. Add onion to skillet and red cabbage: cook and stir over medium-high heat for 6-7 minutes. Add pears and vinegar mixture to skillet. Bring to a boil; reduce heat. Cover and simmer for 5 minutes.
6. Cover with pork chops; reheat. Sprinkle chops with fresh thyme and/or sage, if desired. Serve and enjoy!

PER SERVING

Calories: 218 | Protein: 28.9g | Carbohydrates: 18.7g | Dietary Fiber: 2.7g | Sugar: 13.5g | Fat: 3.3g

Beef & Broccoli Skillet

Prep time: 5 minutes | Cook time: 10 minutes | Serves 4

- 1 lb. lean ground beef
- 3 cups cauliflower rice, cooked
- 2 cups broccoli, chopped
- 4 green onions, sliced
- 1 cup Teriyaki sauce (chapter 16)

1. Cook beef in a large skillet over med-high heat until brown. Add the broccoli and white parts of the onion, cook, stirring for 1 minute.
2. Add the cauliflower and sauce and continue cooking until heated through and broccoli is tender-crisp, about 3-5 minutes. Serve garnished with green parts of the onion.

PER SERVING

Calories: 255 | Total Carbohydrates: 9g | Net Carbohydrates: 6g | Protein: 37g | Fat: 7g | Suger: 3g | Fiber: 3g

Lamb and Mushroom Cheese Burgers

Prep time: 15 minutes | Cook time: 15 minutes | Serves 4

- 8 ounces (227 g) grass-fed ground lamb
- 8 ounces (227 g) brown mushrooms, finely chopped
- ¼ teaspoon salt
- ¼ teaspoon freshly ground black pepper
- ¼ cup crumbled goat cheese
- 1 tablespoon minced fresh basil

1. In a large mixing bowl, combine the lamb, mushrooms, salt, and pepper, and mix well.
2. In a small bowl, mix the goat cheese and basil.
3. Form the lamb mixture into 4 patties, reserving about ½ cup of the mixture in the bowl. In each patty, make an indentation in the center and fill with 1 tablespoon of the goat cheese mixture. Use the reserved meat mixture to close the burgers. Press the meat firmly to hold together.
4. Heat the barbecue or a large skillet over medium-high heat. Add the burgers and cook for 5 to 7 minutes on each side, until cooked through. Serve.

PER SERVING

Calories: 172 | Fat: 13.1g | Protein: 11.1g | Carbohydrates: 2.9g | Fiber: 0g | Sugar: 1g | Sodium: 155mg

Easy Beef Curry

Prep time: 15 minutes | Cook time: 10 minutes | Serves 6

- 1 tablespoon extra-virgin olive oil
- 1 small onion, thinly sliced
- 2 teaspoons minced fresh ginger
- 3 garlic cloves, minced
- 2 teaspoons ground coriander
- 1 teaspoon ground cumin
- 1 jalapeño or serrano pepper, slit lengthwise but not all the way through
- ¼ teaspoon ground turmeric
- ¼ teaspoon salt
- 1 pound grass-fed sirloin tip steak, top round steak, or top sirloin steak, cut into bite-size pieces
- 2 tablespoons chopped fresh cilantro

1. In a large skillet, heat the oil over medium high. Add the onion, and cook for 3 to 5 minutes until browned and softened. Add the ginger and garlic, stirring continuously until fragrant, about 30 seconds.
2. In a small bowl, mix the coriander, cumin, jalapeño, turmeric, and salt. Add the spice mixture to the skillet and stir continuously for 1 minute. Deglaze the skillet with about ¼ cup of water.
3. Add the beef and stir continuously for about 5 minutes until well-browned yet still medium rare. Remove the jalapeño. Serve topped with the cilantro.

PER SERVING

Calories: 140 | Total Fat: 7g | Protein: 18g | Carbohydrates: 3g | Fiber: 1g | Sugar: 1g | Sodium: 141mg

BBQ Pork Tacos

Prep time: 20 minutes | Cook time: 6 hours | Serves 16

- 2 lb. pork shoulder, trim off excess fat
- 2 onions, diced fine
- 2 cups cabbages, shredded
- 16 (6-inch) low carb whole wheat tortillas
- 4 chipotle peppers in adobo sauce, pureed
- 1 cup light barbecue sauce
- 2 cloves garlic, diced fine
- 1 ½ tsp paprika

1. In a medium bowl, whisk together garlic, barbecue sauce and chipotles, cover and chill.
2. Place pork in the crock pot. Cover and cook on low 8-10 hours, or on high 4-6 hours.
3. Transfer pork to a cutting board. Use two forks and shred the pork, discarding the fat. Place pork back in the crock pot. Sprinkle with paprika then pour the barbecue sauce over mixture.
4. To assemble the tacos: place about ¼ cup of pork on warmed tortilla. Top with cabbage and onions and serve. Refrigerate any leftover pork up to 3 days.

PER SERVING

Calories: 265 | Total Carbohydrates: 14g | Net Carbohydrates: 5g | Protein: 17g | Fat: 14g | Suger: 3g | Fiber: 9g

Caribbean Bowls

Prep time: 10 minutes | Cook time: 45 minutes | Serves 4

- 1 teaspoon of crushed red pepper
- 1/2 teaspoon of ground cinnamon
- 1/2 teaspoon of ground cloves
- 2 teaspoons onion powder
- 1 teaspoon of sugar
- 1 teaspoon of crushed dried thyme
- 1/4 teaspoon of black pepper
- 1/4 teaspoon of orange zest
- 1 tablespoon of orange juice
- 1/8 teaspoon of salt
- 1 tablespoon of olive oil
- 1 tablespoon of white wine vinegar
- 1 tablespoon of lime juice
- 1-1/2 tablespoons water
- 1/2 of a 15-ounces can (3/4 cup) of reduced-sodium black beans, rinsed & drained
- 1/2 cup uncooked regular brown rice
- salt
- 1/2 teaspoon Jamaican Jerk Seasoning
- 1/2 fresh jalapeño chili pepper, seeded (if desired) and finely chopped
- 1 pound natural pork tenderloin, trimmed and cut into 1-inch pieces
- 2 teaspoons olive oil
- 1/4 teaspoon black pepper
- 1 cup chopped fresh pineapple
- 1/2 cup sliced red onion
- 1 avocado, halved, seeded, peeled, and sliced
- Fresh cilantro

1. To prepare the Caribbean Bowls. Cook rice with 1/4 teaspoon of the salt and 1/4 teaspoon of the Jamaican Jerk Seasoning according to package directions. Set it aside.
2. In a medium bowl, combine onion, pineapple, and jalapeño pepper. Set aside.
3. In another medium bowl, toss together meat, 2 teaspoons oil, 1/4 teaspoon salt, 1/2 teaspoon of jerk seasoning, and pepper.
4. Heat a 10-inch nonstick skillet over medium-high.
5. Add meat, half at a time, and cook 5 to 6 minutes or until slightly pink in the center.
6. Add the water. Cook 1 to 2 minutes more or until liquid evaporates, stirring to scrape up crusty brown bits and coat meat.
7. Stir beans into cooked rice. Divide meat, rice mixture, and pineapple mixture among individual bowls. Drizzle with vinaigrette and top with avocado and cilantro.

PER SERVING

Calories: 401 | Protein: 29.1g | Carbohydrates: 39.8g | Dietary Fiber: 6.1g | Sugar: 8.3g | Fat: 14.2g

Beef & Veggie Quesadillas

Prep time: 15 minutes | Cook time: 10 minutes | Serves 4

- ¾ lb. lean ground beef
- 2 tomatoes, seeded and diced
- 1 onion, diced
- 1 zucchini, grated
- 1 carrot, grated
- ¾ cup mushrooms, diced
- ½ cup mozzarella cheese, grated
- ¼ cup cilantro, diced
- 4 8-inch whole wheat tortillas, warmed
- 2 cloves garlic, diced
- 2 tsp chili powder
- ¼ tsp salt
- ¼ tsp hot pepper sauce
- Nonstick cooking spray

1. Heat oven to 400 degrees. Spray a large baking sheet with cooking spray.
2. Cook beef and onions in a large nonstick skillet over medium heat, until beef is no longer pink, drain fat. Transfer to a bowl and keep warm.
3. Add the mushrooms, zucchini, carrot, garlic, chili powder, salt and pepper sauce to the skillet and cook until vegetables are tender.
4. Stir in the tomatoes, cilantro and beef.
5. Lay the tortillas on the prepared pan. Cover half of each with beef mixture, and top with cheese. Fold other half over filling. Bake 5 minutes. Flip over and bake 5-6 minute more or until cheese has melted. Cut into wedges and serve.

PER SERVING

Calories: 319 | Total Carbohydrates: 31g | Net Carbohydrates: 26g | Protein: 33g | Fat: 7g | Suger: 5g | Fiber: 5g

Asian Beef Bowls

Prep time: 15 minutes | Cook time: 15 minutes | Serves 4

- 1 lb. lean ground beef
- 1 bunch green onions, sliced
- ¼ cup fresh ginger, grated
- Cauliflower Rice
- ¼ cup toasted sesame oil
- 5 cloves garlic, diced fine
- 2 tbsp. light soy sauce
- 2 tsp sesame seeds

1. Heat oil in a large, cast iron skillet over high heat. Add all but 2 tablespoons, of the onions and cook until soft and starting to brown, about 5 minutes.
2. Add beef, and cook, breaking up with a spatula, until no longer pink. About 8 minutes.
3. Add remaining Ingredients and simmer 2-3 minutes, stirring frequently. Serve over hot cauliflower rice garnished with sesame seeds and reserved green onions.

PER SERVING

Calories: 383 | Total Carbohydrates: 24g | Net Carbohydrates: 22g | Protein: 40g | Fat: 21g | Suger: 191g | Fiber: 2g

Steak with Asparagus

Prep time: 20 minutes | Cook time: 30 minutes | Serves 2

- olive oil spray
- 2 pounds flank steak, cut into 6 pieces
- Kosher salt and black pepper, to taste
- 2 minced garlic cloves
- 4 cups asparagus
- ½ cup tamari sauce
- 3 bell peppers, sliced
- ⅓ cup beef broth, low-sodium
- 1 tablespoon of unsalted butter
- ¼ cup balsamic vinegar

1. Rub salt and pepper on steak liberally.
2. In a Ziploc bag, mix garlic and tamari sauce, then place steak in it, toss well and seal the bag. Let it marinate in the refrigerator for 1 hour or up to overnight.
3. Divide the bell peppers and asparagus in the center of the steak. Roll the steak to seal the vegetables inside and secure well with toothpicks.
4. Preheat the air fryer. Spray the steak with olive oil spray. And place steaks in the air fryer.
5. Cook for almost 15 minutes at 400 degrees F or more till steaks are cooked Take the cooked steak out from the air fryer basket and let it rest for five minutes Remove prepared steak bundles and allow them to rest for almost 5 minutes before serving/slicing.
6. Meanwhile, add butter, balsamic vinegar, and broth over medium flame. Mix well and reduce it by half. Add salt and black pepper to taste.
7. 1pour over steaks right before serving.

PER SERVING

Calories: 471 | Total Carbohydrates: 20g | Net Carbohydrates: 1g | Protein: 29g | Fat: 15g | Suger: 6g | Fiber: 3g

The Complete Diabetic Cookbook for Beginners | 39

Bunless Sloppy Joes

Prep time: 15 minutes | Cook time: 40 minutes | Serves 6

- 6 small sweet potatoes
- 1 pound lean ground beef
- 1 onion, finely chopped
- 1 carrot, finely chopped
- ¼ cup finely chopped mushrooms
- ¼ cup finely chopped red bell pepper
- 3 garlic cloves, minced
- 2 teaspoons Worcestershire sauce
- 1 tablespoon white wine vinegar
- 1 (15-ounce) can low-sodium tomato sauce
- 2 tablespoons tomato paste

1. Preheat the oven to 400°F. Place the sweet potatoes in a single layer in a baking dish. Bake for 25 to 40 minutes, depending on the size, until they are soft and cooked through.
2. While the sweet potatoes are baking, in a large skillet, cook the beef over medium heat until it's browned, breaking it apart into small pieces as you stir. Add the onion, carrot, mushrooms, bell pepper, and garlic, and sauté briefly for 1 minute. Stir in the Worcestershire sauce, vinegar, tomato sauce, and tomato paste. Bring to a simmer, reduce the heat, and cook for 5 minutes for the flavors to meld.
3. Scoop ½ cup of the meat mixture on top of each baked potato and serve.

PER SERVING

Calories: 372 | Total Fat: 19g | Protein: 16g | Carbohydrates: 34g | Fiber: 6g | Sugar: 13g | Sodium: 161mg

Beef Kabobs with Vegetables

Prep time: 30 minutes | Cook time: 10 minutes | Serves 4

- 2 tablespoons soy sauce
- 4 cups beef chuck ribs, sliced into one-inch pieces
- ⅓ cup low-fat sour cream
- half onion
- 8 skewers: 6 inches
- 1 bell pepper, diced

1. In a suitable mixing bowl, add soy sauce and sour cream, mix well. Add the beef chunks, mix well, and let it marinate for half an hour or more.
2. Cut onion and bell pepper into one-inch pieces. In water, soak skewers for ten minutes. Thread bell peppers, onions, and beef on skewers; alternatively, sprinkle with black pepper Let it cook for almost 10 minutes in a preheated air fryer at 400 degrees F, flip halfway through.
3. Serve with yogurt dipping sauce.

PER SERVING

Calories: 268 | Total Carbohydrates: 15g | Net Carbohydrates: 1g | Protein: 20g | Fat: 10g | Suger: 6g | Fiber: 3g

Easy Rib-Eye Steak

Prep time: 5 minutes | Cook time: 14 minutes | Serves 2

- 2 medium-sized lean rib-eye steaks
- salt and black pepper, to taste

1. At 400 degrees F, preheat your Air Fryer.
2. Pat dry steaks with paper towels. Rub the steaks with the seasonings generously on both sides of the steak. Place the prepared steaks in the air fryer basket. Cook according to the rareness you want. Or cook for 14 minutes and flip after halftime.
3. Take it out from the air fryer basket and let it rest for almost 5 minutes. Serve with microgreen salad.

PER SERVING

Calories: 470 | Total Carbohydrates: 23g | Net Carbohydrates: 1g | Protein: 47g | Fat: 31g | Suger: 6g | Fiber: 3g

Cherry-Glazed Lamb Chops

Prep time: 10 minutes | Cook time: 20 minutes | Serves 4

- 4 (4-ounce / 113-g) lamb chops
- 1½ teaspoons chopped fresh rosemary
- ¼ teaspoon salt
- ¼ teaspoon freshly ground black pepper
- 1 cup frozen cherries, thawed
- ¼ cup dry red wine
- 2 tablespoons orange juice
- 1 teaspoon extra-virgin olive oil

1. Season the lamb chops with the rosemary, salt, and pepper.
2. In a small saucepan over medium-low heat, combine the cherries, red wine, and orange juice, and simmer, stirring regularly, until the sauce thickens, 8 to 10 minutes.
3. Heat a large skillet over medium-high heat. When the pan is hot, add the olive oil to lightly coat the bottom.
4. Cook the lamb chops for 3 to 4 minutes on each side until well-browned yet medium rare.
5. Serve, topped with the cherry glaze.

PER SERVING

Calories: 355 | Fat: 27.1g | Protein: 19.8g | Carbohydrates: 5.9g | Fiber: 1g | Sugar: 4g | Sodium: 200mg

Beef and Zucchini Lasagna

Cook time: 1 hour 30 minutes | Serves 1

- 16 ounces Ground beef, 92%
- 2 medium Zucchini
- 4½ ounces Onion
- 2 cloves Garlic
- 1 Serrano chili
- 3 Tomatoes (skinned)
- 5½ ounces Mushrooms
- ½ cube Chicken bouillon
- ½ cup Low-fat mozzarella (shredded)
- 1 teaspoon Paprika
- 1 teaspoon Dried thyme
- 1 teaspoon Dried basil
- as per taste Salt
- as per taste Pepper
- Cooking spray

1. Start by making ½-inch slices of zucchini using a julienne peeler.
2. Once done, sprinkle all the zucchini slices with salt. Set aside for about 10 minutes.
3. Use a paper towel to blot excess water from the zucchini slices. Place them on a baking sheet.
4. Once done, place the broiled zucchini slices on kitchen paper towels.
5. Chop the onions, chili, garlic, mushrooms, and skinned tomatoes roughly. Set them aside.
6. Take a deep nonstick skillet and grease it using cooking spray. Place it over a medium-high flame.
7. Now add the onion, garlic, and chili to the heated skillet and cook for about 1 minute.
8. Toss in the mushrooms and tomatoes. Sauté the veggies for another 4 minutes. Turn off the heat and empty the ingredients into a bowl.
9. Place the same skillet over a medium flame and add in the ground beef. Sprinkle with paprika and cook until the meat turns brown.
10. Return the cooked vegetables to the pan and mix well. Also add in the chicken bouillon, paprika, dried thyme, and dried basil. Mix well and cook for about 25 minutes over a low flame.
11. In the meantime, let the oven preheat by setting the temperature to 375°F.
12. Take a deep glass baking dish and line it with parchment paper.
13. Further layer the bottom of the dish with 1/3 of the zucchini slices. Now evenly spread the meat mixture over the zucchini slices. Repeat the process with the remaining zucchini and meat mixture. (There should be a minimum of 3 layers.)
14. Sprinkle the shredded mozzarella on the top of the final layer.
15. Place the baking dish in the preheated oven and bake for about 35 minutes.
16. Serve hot!

PER SERVING

Fat: 7.9g | Protein: 30.4g | Carbohydrates: 12.3g

Chapter 8
Fish and Seafood

Tomato Tuna Melts
Prep time: 5 minutes | Cook time: 5 minutes | Serves 2

- 1 (5-ounce) can chunk light tuna packed in water, drained
- 2 tablespoons plain nonfat Greek yogurt
- 2 teaspoons freshly squeezed lemon juice
- 2 tablespoons finely chopped celery
- 1 tablespoon finely chopped red onion
- Pinch cayenne pepper
- 1 large tomato, cut into ¾-inch-thick rounds
- ½ cup shredded cheddar cheese

1. Preheat the broiler to high.
2. In a medium bowl, combine the tuna, yogurt, lemon juice, celery, red onion, and cayenne pepper. Stir well.
3. Arrange the tomato slices on a baking sheet. Top each with some tuna salad and cheddar cheese.
4. Broil for 3 to 4 minutes until the cheese is melted and bubbly. Serve.

PER SERVING
Calories: 243 | Total Fat: 10g | Protein: 30g | Carbohydrates: 7g | Fiber: 1g | Sugar: 2g | Sodium: 444mg

Peppercorn-Crusted Baked Salmon
Prep time: 5 minutes | Cook time: 20 minutes | Serves 4

- Nonstick cooking spray
- ½ teaspoon freshly ground black pepper
- ¼ teaspoon salt
- Zest and juice of ½ lemon
- ¼ teaspoon dried thyme
- 1 pound salmon fillet

1. Preheat the oven to 425°F. Spray a baking sheet with nonstick cooking spray.
2. In a small bowl, combine the pepper, salt, lemon zest and juice, and thyme. Stir to combine.
3. Place the salmon on the prepared baking sheet, skin-side down. Spread the seasoning mixture evenly over the fillet.
4. Bake for 15 to 20 minutes, depending on the thickness of the fillet, until the flesh flakes easily.

PER SERVING
Calories: 163 | Total Fat: 7g | Protein: 23g | Carbohydrates: 1g | Fiber: 0g | Sugar: 0g | Sodium: 167mg

Celery Fish Salad
Prep time: 20 minutes | Cook time: 20 minutes | Serves 4

- 6 cups of thinly sliced celery
- 1/2 cup of sliced med. onion
- 1/2 cup of diet mayonnaise
- 1 teaspoon of salt
- 1/4 teaspoon of pepper
- 1 1/2 cup of orange sections

1. Combine all ingredients except fish and orange.
2. Mix well. Add fish and orange and toss to combine.
3. Serve on lettuce leaves.
4. Garnish with radish roses and tomato wedges.

PER SERVING
Calories: 331 | Fat: 10g | Cholesterol: 111mg | Sodium: 687mg | Carbohydrates: 47g | Sugar: 6g | Fiber: 27g | Protein: 36g

Coastal Creole Shrimp
Prep time: 15 minutes | Cook time: 35 minutes | Serves 4

- 8 to 10 shrimp each
- 2 cups Vegetable or Chicken Broth (here) or store-bought low-sodium broth, divided
- 1 medium green bell pepper, roughly chopped
- 1 medium fennel bulb, cored and roughly chopped
- 1 medium onion, finely chopped
- 2 celery stalks, finely chopped
- 6 garlic cloves, pressed and chopped
- 2 teaspoons Creole Seasoning
- 3 cups chopped tomatoes
- 1 teaspoon Pepper Sauce
- 3 bay leaves
- 1 dash Worcestershire sauce
- 2 pounds medium shrimp, shelled and deveined

1. In a large cast iron skillet, bring 1 cup of broth to a simmer over medium heat.
2. Add the bell pepper, fennel, onion, celery, and garlic. Cook, stirring often, taking care that the vegetables do not char, for 5 to 7 minutes, or until soft.
3. Add the Creole seasoning and cook, continuing to stir so the spices do not burn, for 5 minutes, or until a soft paste is formed.
4. Add the remaining 1 cup of broth, the tomatoes, pepper sauce, bay leaves, cayenne, and Worcestershire sauce.
5. Reduce the heat to low and cook, stirring often, for 10 minutes, or until the flavors marry.
6. Add the shrimp and cook for 3 to 5 minutes, or until they are evenly pink throughout. (Take care not to overcook the shrimp, or they will turn rubbery.) Discard the bay leaves before serving.

PER SERVING
Calories: 304 | Total Fat: 3g | Cholesterol: 329mg | Sodium: 498mg | Total Carbohydrates: 17g | Sugar: 6g | Fiber: 5g | Protein: 51g

Jumpin' Jambalaya

Prep time: 20 minutes | Cook time: 1 hour | Serves 4

- 1 thigh, 4 shrimp, and ¼ cup rice each
- 4 cups Chicken Broth (here) or store-bought low-sodium chicken broth, divided
- 1 pound medium shrimp, shelled and deveined
- 2 tablespoons Creole Seasoning, divided
- 1 medium yellow onion, chopped
- 2 celery stalks including leaves, chopped
- 1 medium green bell pepper, roughly chopped
- 3 garlic cloves, minced
- 1 teaspoon Pepper Sauce
- 4 boneless, skinless chicken thighs
- 2 cups coarsely crushed tomatoes
- 1¼ cups aromatic brown rice
- Freshly ground black pepper

1. In a Dutch oven, bring 1 cup of broth to a simmer over medium heat.
2. Add the shrimp and 1 tablespoon of seasoning and cook for 3 minutes, or until light pink.
3. Using a slotted spoon, remove the shrimp, and set aside.
4. Add ½ cup of broth, the onion, celery, bell pepper, garlic, and pepper sauce, and cook for 2 minutes, or until the vegetables are softened.
5. Add the chicken, remaining 1 tablespoon of seasoning, and ½ cup of broth and cook for 10 minutes, or until the juices run clear.
6. Add the tomatoes and cook for 3 to 5 minutes, or until softened.
7. Add the rice and remaining 2 cups of broth. Season with black pepper.
8. Bring to a boil, then cover. Reduce to a simmer and cook for 40 minutes, or until the rice is tender.
9. Stir in the shrimp and heat through. Serve and enjoy.

PER SERVING

Calories: 495 | Total Fat: 8g | Cholesterol: 317mg | Sodium: 397mg | Total Carbohydrates: 52g | Sugar: 3g | Fiber: 3g | Protein: 54g

Lazy Sushi

Prep time: 5 minutes | Cook time: 5 minutes | Serves 2

- 20 medium fresh shrimp, peeled and deveined
- 1 teaspoon avocado oil
- 1 large cucumber
- 1 avocado
- 2 (4-gram) packages dried nori
- ¼ cup Spicy Asian-Style Sauce

1. Heat a medium skillet over low heat.
2. In a large bowl, toss the shrimp with the oil, then place them into the skillet. Cook for 1 to 2 minutes on each side until they are pink and opaque. Set aside to cool.
3. Cut the cucumber into ¼-inch-thick planks about 2 inches long.
4. Cut the avocado into 10 slices.
5. Arrange half of the shrimp, cucumber, avocado, and nori on each of two plates, and serve with the sauce on the side.

PER SERVING

Calories: 266 | Total Fat: 19g | Protein: 15g | Carbohydrates: 14g | Fiber: 7g | Sugar: 3g | Sodium: 275mg

Roasted Salmon with Honey-Mustard Sauce

Prep time: 5 minutes | Cook time: 20 minutes | Serves 4

- Nonstick cooking spray
- 2 tablespoons whole-grain mustard
- 1 tablespoon honey
- 2 garlic cloves, minced
- ¼ teaspoon salt
- ¼ teaspoon freshly ground black pepper
- 1 pound salmon fillet

1. Preheat the oven to 425°F. Spray a baking sheet with nonstick cooking spray.
2. In a small bowl, whisk together the mustard, honey, garlic, salt, and pepper.
3. Place the salmon fillet on the prepared baking sheet, skin-side down. Spoon the sauce onto the salmon and spread evenly.
4. Roast for 15 to 20 minutes, depending on the thickness of the fillet, until the flesh flakes easily.

PER SERVING

Calories: 186 | Total Fat: 7g | Protein: 23g | Carbohydrates: 6g | Fiber: 0g | Sugar: 4g | Sodium: 312mg

Shrimp Stir-Fry

Prep time: 5 minutes | Cook time: 15 minutes | Serves 4

- ½ cup water
- 2½ tablespoons low-sodium soy sauce
- 2 tablespoons honey
- 1 tablespoon rice vinegar
- ¼ teaspoon garlic powder
- Pinch ground ginger
- 1 tablespoon cornstarch
- 8 cups frozen vegetable stir-fry mix
- 2 tablespoons sesame oil
- 40 medium fresh shrimp, peeled and deveined

1. In a small saucepan, whisk together the water, soy sauce, honey, rice vinegar, garlic powder, and ginger. Add the cornstarch and whisk until fully incorporated. Bring the sauce to a boil over medium heat. Boil for 1 minute to thicken. Remove the sauce from the heat and set aside.
2. Heat a large saucepan over medium-high heat. When hot, put the vegetable stir-fry mix into the pan, and cook for 7 to 10 minutes, stirring occasionally until the water completely evaporates.
3. Reduce the heat to medium-low, add the oil and shrimp, and stir. Cook for about 3 minutes, or until the shrimp are pink and opaque.
4. Add the sauce to the shrimp and vegetables and stir to coat. Cook for 2 minutes more.

PER SERVING

Calories: 297 | Total Fat: 17g | Protein: 24g | Carbohydrates: 14g | Fiber: 2g | Sugar: 9g | Sodium: 454mg

Low Country Boil

Prep time: 15 minutes | Cook time: 10 minutes | Serves 8

- 5 to 8 shrimp, 2 pieces sausage, 1 potato, and 1 piece corn each
- 2 pounds small new potatoes
- 1 pound low-sodium chicken sausage, cut into 2-inch pieces
- 1 pound shell-on medium shrimp, deveined
- ½ cup Not Old Bay Seasoning
- 2 small onions, quartered
- 1 garlic bulb
- 1 celery stalk including leaves, halved
- 2 bay leaves
- 2 cups water
- 4 ears fresh corn, halved
- Lemons, cut into eighths, for serving

1. In an electric pressure cooker, combine the potatoes, sausage, shrimp, seasoning, onions, garlic, celery, and bay leaves. Cover with the water, and top with the corn.
2. Close and lock the lid, and set the pressure valve to sealing.
3. Select the Manual/Pressure Cook setting, and cook for 7 minutes. Once cooking is complete, quick-release the pressure. Carefully remove the lid.
4. Drain the liquid and discard the bay leaves. Transfer the shrimp, sausage, and vegetables to a bowl and serve immediately. Garnish each portion with a lemon wedge (if using).

PER SERVING

Calories: 294 | Total Fat: 6g | Cholesterol: 141mg | Sodium: 451mg | Total Carbohydrates: 39g | Sugar: 4g | Fiber: 5g | Protein: 25g

Fish Tacos

Prep time: 5 minutes | Cook time: 10 minutes | Serves 4

- 2 tablespoons extra-virgin olive oil
- 4 (6-ounce) cod fillets
- 8 (10-inch) yellow corn tortillas
- 2 cups packaged shredded cabbage
- ¼ cup chopped fresh cilantro
- 4 lime wedges
- ½ cup plain low-fat Greek yogurt
- ⅓ cup low-fat mayonnaise
- ½ teaspoon garlic powder
- ½ teaspoon ground cumin

1. Heat a medium skillet over medium-low heat. When hot, pour the oil into the skillet, then add the fish and cover. Cook for 4 minutes, then flip and cook for 4 minutes more.
2. Top each tortilla with one-eighth of the cabbage, sauce, cilantro, and fish. Finish each taco with a squeeze of lime.
3. In a small bowl, whisk together the yogurt, mayonnaise, garlic powder, and cumin.

PER SERVING

Calories: 373 | Total Fat: 13g | Protein: 36g | Carbohydrates: 30g | Fiber: 4g | Sugar: 4g | Sodium: 342mg

Herbed Fish Fillets

Prep time: 5 minutes | Cook time: 20 minutes | Serves 4

- 1 pound of fillets
- 1/2 teaspoon of salt
- Dash of garlic powder
- 1/4 ounces of drained, chopped mushrooms
- 1/8 teaspoon of ground thyme
- 1/2 teaspoon of onion powder
- Dash of black pepper
- 1/2 teaspoon of dried parsley
- 1 tablespoon of nonfat dry milk
- 1 tablespoon of water
- 1/2 teaspoon of lemon juice

1. Sprinkle fish with salt and garlic powder.
2. Mix remaining ingredients and spread over fish.
3. Bake at 375 degrees for 20 mins until fish flakes with a fork. Serve and enjoy!

PER SERVING

Calories: 262 | Protein: 30.2g | Carbohydrates: 3.3g | Dietary Fiber: 1.2g | Sugar: 0.8g | Fat: 15g | Saturated Fat: 2.2g | Cholesterol: 70.9mg

Baked Fish

Prep time: 5 minutes | Cook time: 5 minutes | Serves 4

- 1/4 cup of margarine
- 1 tablespoon of lemon juice
- 1/4 teaspoon of freshly ground pepper
- 1/4 teaspoon of basil
- Any fish fillets

1. Firmly and evenly into the base of the prepared pan, and use the back of a spoon to smooth.
2. Chill while preparing the filling for about 5 minutes, often stirring to stop it from scorching. Serve and enjoy!

PER SERVING

Calories: 241 | Fat: 4g | Protein: 15g | Carbohydrates: 37g | Fiber: 5g | Sugar: 7g

Shrimp Scampi

Prep time: 20 minutes | Cook time: 15 minutes | Serves 4

- 1/2 cup of reconstituted dry butter substitute
- 1/2 teaspoon of salt
- 1/2 teaspoon of garlic powder
- 1/2 teaspoon of parsley
- 1/4 teaspoon of oregano
- 1/4 teaspoon of sweet basil
- 1/8 teaspoon of cayenne pepper
- 1 1/2 cup of fat-free chicken broth
- 1 1/2 tablespoon of lemon juice
- 2 cups of cooked shrimp, peeled and deveined
- 1 tablespoon of cornstarch

1. Combine all ingredients except shrimp and cornstarch.
2. Bring to a boil and add shrimp.
3. Stir in cornstarch to thicken.

PER SERVING

Calories: 209 | Fat: 5.6g | Protein: 17.5g | Carbohydrates: 20g | Fiber: 6g | Sugar: 7.8g | Sodium: 963.8mg | Potassium: 349.7mg

Chapter 9
Vegetable and Side Dishes

Tomato Vegetable Soup

Prep time: 10 minutes | Cook time: 20 minutes | Serves 2

- 2 teaspoons olive oil
- 1 onion, chopped
- 2 celery stalks, chopped
- 1 red bell pepper, seeded and chopped
- 2 teaspoons minced garlic
- 3 cups low-sodium vegetable broth
- 1 (15-ounce) can no-salt-added diced tomatoes
- 1 carrot, peeled and chopped
- 1 cup small cauliflower florets
- ½ cup green beans, trimmed and cut into 1-inch pieces
- Sea salt
- Freshly ground black pepper

1. In a large stockpot, heat the oil over medium-high heat. Sauté the onion, celery, bell pepper, and garlic for about 5 minutes, until softened.
2. Add the broth, tomatoes and their juices, carrot, cauliflower, and green beans to the pot. Bring the soup to a boil, reduce the heat to low, and simmer for about 15 minutes, until the vegetables are crisp-tender.
3. Season with salt and pepper and serve.

PER SERVING

Calories: 160 | Total Fat: 6g | Saturated Fat: 1g | Sodium: 175mg | Carbohydrates: 26g | Sugar: 13g | Fiber: 10g | Protein: 5g

Chipotle Twice-Baked Sweet Potatoes

Prep time: 20 minutes | Cook time: 1 hour 25 minutes | Serves 4

- 4 small sweet potatoes (about 1¾ lb)
- ¼ cup fat-free half-and-half
- 1 chipotle chile in adobo sauce (from 7-oz can), finely chopped
- 1 teaspoon adobo sauce (from can of chipotle chiles)
- ½ teaspoon salt
- 8 teaspoons reduced-fat sour cream
- 4 teaspoons chopped fresh cilantro

1. Heat oven to 375°F. Gently scrub potatoes but do not peel. Pierce potatoes several times with fork to allow steam to escape while potatoes bake. Bake about 45 minutes or until potatoes are tender when pierced in center with a fork.
2. When potatoes are cool enough to handle, cut lengthwise down through center of potato to within ½ inch of ends and bottom. Carefully scoop out inside, leaving thin shell. In medium bowl, mash potatoes, half-and-half, chile, adobo sauce and salt with potato masher or electric mixer on low speed until light and fluffy.
3. Increase oven temperature to 400°F. In 13x9-inch pan, place potato shells. Divide potato mixture evenly among shells. Bake uncovered 20 minutes or until potato mixture is golden brown and heated through.
4. Just before serving, top each potato with 2 teaspoons sour cream and 1 teaspoon cilantro.

PER SERVING

Calories: 140 | Total Fat: 1.5g | Cholesterol: 0mg | Sodium: 400mg | Total Carbohydrates: 27g | Sugar: 9g | Fiber: 4g | Protein: 3g

Broccoli and Squash Medley

Prep time: 30 minutes | Cook time: 30 minutes | Serves 14

- 2 bags (12 oz each) frozen broccoli cuts
- 2 cups cubed (½ inch) peeled butternut squash (1½ lb)
- ½ cup orange juice
- 1 tablespoon butter or margarine, melted
- ½ cup sweetened dried cranberries
- ½ cup finely chopped pecans, toasted*
- 1 tablespoon grated orange peel
- ½ teaspoon salt

1. Cook broccoli as directed on bag; set aside.
2. Meanwhile, in 12-inch skillet, cook squash in orange juice over medium-low heat 8 to 10 minutes, stirring frequently, until tender but firm.
3. Stir in butter, broccoli, cranberries, pecans, orange peel and salt; toss to coat. Serve immediately.
4. To toast pecans, sprinkle in ungreased heavy skillet. Cook over medium heat 5 to 7 minutes, stirring frequently until pecans begin to brown, then stirring constantly until light brown.

PER SERVING

Calories: 80 | Total Fat: 4g | Cholesterol: 0mg | Sodium: 125mg | Total Carbohydrates: 10g | Sugar: 5g | Fiber: 2g | Protein: 1g

Herb Seasoned Broccoli

Prep time: 10 minutes | Cook time: 6 minutes | Serves 2

- 1/2 cup of water
- 1 packet of instant chicken broth and seasoning mix
- 2 cups of broccoli spears
- 1/2 teaspoon of marjoram
- 1/2 teaspoon of basil
- 1/4 teaspoon of onion powder
- Dash of nutmeg
- 1 tablespoon of margarine
- 2 teaspoons of lemon juice

1. Combine water and broth mixture.
2. Add broccoli, sprinkle with seasonings.
3. Cover, bring to boil, simmer 6 mins until tender. Drain.
4. Divide between plates. Top with margarine and lemon juice. Serve and enjoy!

PER SERVING

Calories: 12 | Protein: 0.4g | Carbohydrates: 2.9g | Dietary Fiber: 0.7g | Sugar: 1.7g

Navy Bean Soup with Spinach
Prep time: 10 minutes | **Cook time:** 20 minutes | **Serves 2**

- 2 teaspoons olive oil
- 1 onion, chopped
- 2 celery stalks, diced
- 2 teaspoons minced garlic
- 3 cups sodium-free vegetable broth
- 1 (15-ounce) can low-sodium great northern beans, drained and rinsed
- 2 carrots, peeled and diced
- 1 tomato, diced
- 1 cup baby spinach
- 2 teaspoons chopped fresh thyme, or 1 teaspoon dried thyme
- Sea salt
- Freshly ground black pepper

1. In a medium stockpot, heat the oil over medium-high heat. Sauté the onion, celery, and garlic for about 5 minutes, until softened.
2. Add the broth, beans, carrots, and tomato and bring to a boil. Reduce the heat to low and simmer for about 13 minutes, until the carrots are tender. Add the spinach and thyme and simmer for an additional 2 minutes.
3. Season with salt and pepper and serve.

PER SERVING

Calories: 293 | Total Fat: 5g | Saturated Fat: 1g | Sodium: 165mg | Carbohydrates: 50g | Sugar: 11g | Fiber: 15g | Protein: 14g

Zucchini Basil Muffins
Prep time: 10 minutes | **Cook time:** 15 minutes | **Serves 10-18**

- 2 eggs
- 3/4 cup of milk
- 2/3 cup of oil
- 2 cups of flour
- 1 teaspoon Sugar substitute
- 1 tablespoon of baking powder
- 1 teaspoon of salt
- 2 cups of shredded zucchini
- 2 tablespoons of minced basil
- 1/4 cup of grated Parmesan cheese

1. Beat the eggs in a bowl. Stir in oil and milk.
2. Combine sugar, flour, baking powder, and salt.
3. Stir the dry ingredients into the egg mixture just until the flour is moistened.
4. The batter should not be completely smooth. Gently mix in zucchini and basil.
5. Fill greased muffin cups about 3/4 full.
6. Remove from pan. Makes 10-18 muffins depending on the size of the pan. Serve and enjoy!

PER SERVING

Calories: 299 | Fat: 15g | Cholesterol: 73mg | Carbohydrates: 23g | Fiber: 4g | Protein: 18g

Molted Vegetable Salad
Prep time: 10 minutes | **Cook time:** 0 minutes | **Serves 12**

- 1 packet of sugar-free lemon Jello
- 2 cups of boiling water
- 2 tablespoons of lemon juice
- 2/3 cup of cabbage, chopped
- 2/3 cup of green pepper, chopped
- 2 slices pimiento
- Lettuce leaves

1. Dissolve gelatin in boiling water.
2. Add lemon juice and chopped vegetables.
3. Serve on lettuce leaves with low-calorie dressing.

PER SERVING

Calories: 220 | Fat: 13g | Protein: 6g | Carbohydrates: 21g | Fiber: 2g | Sugar: 1g

Chili Relleno Casserole
Prep time: 5 minutes | **Cook time:** 35 minutes | **Serves 8**

- 3 eggs
- 1 cup Monterey jack pepper cheese, grated
- 3/4 cup half-n-half
- ½ cup cheddar cheese, grated
- 2 (7 oz.) cans whole green chilies, drain well
- ½ tsp salt
- Nonstick cooking spray

1. Heat oven to 350 degrees. Spray an 8-inch baking pan with cooking spray.
2. Slice each chili down one long side and lay flat.
3. Arrange half the chilies in the prepared baking pan, skin side down, in single layer.
4. Sprinkle with the pepper cheese and top with remaining chilies, skin side up.
5. In a small bowl, beat eggs, salt, and half-n-half. Pour over chilies. Top with cheddar cheese.
6. Bake 35 minutes, or until top is golden brown. Let rest 10 minutes before serving.

PER SERVING

Calories: 295 | Total Carbohydrates: 36g | Net Carbohydrates: 22g | Protein: 13g | Fat: 13g | Suger: 21g | Fiber: 14g

Baked Tomatoes

Prep time: 10 minutes | Cook time: 10 minutes | Serves 1

- 1 medium-sized tomato
- Other seasonings to taste
- 1/2 teaspoon of chopped parsley
- Salt & pepper
- 1/2 teaspoon of chopped onion
- 1/2 teaspoon of sage or chives

1. Wash tomatoes and cut out stem end.
2. Place in an ovenproof dish with a bit of water in the bottom.
3. Sprinkle with toppings of your choice.
4. Bake in a moderate oven (375 degrees) until the tomato is tender but not so soft that it falls apart. About 15 to 20 minutes. Serve.

PER SERVING

Calories: 90 | Fat: 3.5g | Protein: 1g | Carbohydrates: 14g | Fiber: 4g | Sugar: 5g

Asian Fried Eggplant

Prep time: 10 minutes | Cook time: 40 minutes | Serves 4

- 1 large eggplant, sliced into fourths
- 3 green onions, diced, green tips only
- 1 tsp fresh ginger, peeled & diced fine
- ¼ cup + 1 tsp cornstarch
- 1½ tbsp. soy sauce
- 1½ tbsp. sesame oil
- 1 tbsp. vegetable oil
- 1 tbsp. fish sauce
- 2 tsp Splenda
- ¼ tsp salt

1. Place eggplant on paper towels and sprinkle both sides with salt. Let for 1 hour to remove excess moisture. Pat dry with more paper towels.
2. In a small bowl, whisk together soy sauce, sesame oil, fish sauce, Splenda, and 1 teaspoon cornstarch.
3. Coat both sides of the eggplant with the ¼ cup cornstarch, use more if needed.
4. Heat oil in a large skillet, over med-high heat. Add ½ the ginger and 1 green onion, then lay 2 slices of eggplant on top. Use ½ the sauce mixture to lightly coat both sides of the eggplant. Cook 8-10 minutes per side. Repeat.
5. Serve garnished with remaining green onions.

PER SERVING

Calories: 155 | Total Carbohydrates: 18g | Net Carbohydrates: 13g | Protein: 2g | Fat: 9g | Suger: 6g | Fiber: 5g

Butternut Fritters

Prep time: 15 minutes | Cook time: 15 minutes | Serves 6

- 5 cup butternut squash, grated
- 2 large eggs
- 1 tbsp. fresh sage, diced fine
- 2/3 cup flour
- 2 tbsp. olive oil
- Salt and pepper, to taste

1. Heat oil in a large skillet over med-high heat.
2. In a large bowl, combine squash, eggs, sage and salt and pepper to taste. Fold in flour.
3. Drop ¼ cup mixture into skillet, keeping fritters at least 1 inch apart. Cook till golden brown on both sides, about 2 minutes per side.
4. Transfer to paper towel lined plate. Repeat. Serve immediately with your favorite dipping sauce.

PER SERVING

Calories: 164 | Total Carbohydrates: 24g | Net Carbohydrates: 21g | Protein: 4g | Fat: 6g | Suger: 3g | Fiber: 3g

Cauliflower Mushroom Risotto

Prep time: 10 minutes | Cook time: 30 minutes | Serves 2

- 1 medium head cauliflower, grated
- 8 oz. Porcini mushrooms, sliced
- 1 yellow onion, diced fine
- 2 cup low sodium vegetable broth
- 2 tsp garlic, diced fine
- 2 tsp white wine vinegar
- Salt & pepper, to taste
- Olive oil cooking spray

1. Heat oven to 350 degrees. Line a baking sheet with foil.
2. Place the mushrooms on the prepared pan and spray with cooking spray. Sprinkle with salt and toss to coat. Bake 10-12 minutes, or until golden brown and the mushrooms start to crisp.
3. Spray a large skillet with cooking spray and place over med-high heat. Add onion and cook, stirring frequently, until translucent, about 3-4 minutes. Add garlic and cook 2 minutes, until golden.
4. Add the cauliflower and cook 1 minute, stirring.
5. Place the broth in a saucepan and bring to a simmer. Add to the skillet, ¼ cup at a time, mixing well after each addition.
6. Stir in vinegar. Reduce heat to low and let simmer, 4-5 minutes, or until most of the liquid has evaporated. Spoon cauliflower mixture onto plates, or in bowls, and top with mushrooms. Serve.

PER SERVING

Calories: 134 | Total Carbohydrates: 22g | Protein: 10g | Fat: 0g | Suger: 5g | Fiber: 2g

Chapter 10
Soups, Salads, and Sandwiches

Asian Noodle Salad

Prep time: 30 minutes | Serves 4

- 2 carrots, sliced thin
- 2 radish, sliced thin
- 1 English cucumber, sliced thin
- 1 mango, julienned
- 1 bell pepper, julienned
- 1 small serrano pepper, seeded and sliced thin
- 1 bag tofu Shirataki Fettuccini noodles
- ¼ cup lime juice
- ¼ cup fresh basil, chopped
- ¼ cup fresh cilantro, chopped
- 2 tbsp. fresh mint, chopped
- 2 tbsp. rice vinegar
- 2 tbsp. sweet chili sauce
- 2 tbsp. roasted peanuts finely chopped
- 1 tbsp. Splenda
- ½ tsp sesame oil

1. In a large bowl, place radish, cucumbers, and carrots. Add vinegar, coconut sugar, and lime juice and stir to coat the vegetables. Cover and chill 1520 minutes.
2. remove the noodles from the package and rinse under cold water. Cut into smaller pieces. Pat dry with paper towels.
3. To assemble the salad. Remove the vegetables from the marinade, reserving marinade, and place in a large mixing bowl. Add noodles, mango, bell pepper, chili, and herbs.
4. In a small bowl, combine 2 tablespoons marinade with the chili sauce and sesame oil. Pour over salad and toss to coat. Top with peanuts and serve.

PER SERVING

Calories: 158 | Total Carbohydrates: 30g | Net Carbohydrates: 24g | Protein: 4g | Fat: 4g | Suger: 19g | Fiber: 6g

Baked "Potato" Salad

Prep time: 15 minutes | Cook time: 15 minutes | Serves 8

- 2 lb. cauliflower, separated into small florets
- 6-8 slices bacon, chopped and fried crisp
- 6 boiled eggs, cooled, peeled, and chopped
- 1 cup sharp cheddar cheese, grated
- ½ cup green onion, sliced
- 1 cup reduced-fat mayonnaise
- 2 tsp yellow mustard
- 1 ½ tsp onion powder, divided
- Salt and fresh-ground black pepper to taste

1. Place cauliflower in a vegetable steamer, or a pot with a steamer insert, and steam 5-6 minutes.
2. Drain the cauliflower and set aside.
3. In a small bowl, whisk together mayonnaise, mustard, 1 teaspoon onion powder, salt, and pepper.
4. Pat cauliflower dry with paper towels and place in a large mixing bowl. Add eggs, salt, pepper, remaining ½ teaspoon onion powder, then dressing. Mix gently to combine Ingredients together.
5. Fold in the bacon, cheese, and green onion. Serve warm or cover and chill before serving.

PER SERVING

Calories: 247| Total Carbohydrates: 8g | Net Carbohydrates: 5g | Protein: 17g | Fat: 17g | Suger: 3g | Fiber: 3g

Comforting Summer Squash Soup with Crispy Chickpeas

Prep time: 10 minutes | Cook time: 20 minutes | Serves 4

- 1 (15-ounce) can low-sodium chickpeas, drained and rinsed
- 1 teaspoon extra-virgin olive oil, plus 1 tablespoon
- ¼ teaspoon smoked paprika
- Pinch salt, plus ½ teaspoon
- 3 medium zucchini, coarsely chopped
- 3 cups low-sodium vegetable broth
- ½ onion, diced
- 3 garlic cloves, minced
- 2 tablespoons plain low-fat Greek yogurt
- Freshly ground black pepper

1. Preheat the oven to 425°F. Line a baking sheet with parchment paper.
2. In a medium mixing bowl, toss the chickpeas with 1 teaspoon of olive oil, the smoked paprika, and a pinch salt. Transfer to the prepared baking sheet and roast until crispy, about 20 minutes, stirring once. Set aside.
3. Meanwhile, in a medium pot, heat the remaining 1 tablespoon of oil over medium heat.
4. Add the zucchini, broth, onion, and garlic to the pot, and bring to a boil. Reduce the heat to a simmer, and cook until the zucchini and onion are tender, about 20 minutes.
5. In a blender jar, or using an immersion blender, purée the soup. Return to the pot.
6. Add the yogurt, remaining ½ teaspoon of salt, and pepper, and stir well. Serve topped with the roasted chickpeas.

PER SERVING

Calories: 188 | Total Fat: 7g | Protein: 8g | Carbohydrates: 24g | Fiber: 7g | Sugar: 7g | Sodium: 528mg

Beef and Mushroom Barley Soup
Prep time: 10 minutes | Cook time: 1 hour 20 minutes | Serves 6

- 1 pound beef stew meat, cubed
- ¼ teaspoon salt
- ¼ teaspoon freshly ground black pepper
- 1 tablespoon extra-virgin olive oil
- 8 ounces sliced mushrooms
- 1 onion, chopped
- 2 carrots, chopped
- 3 celery stalks, chopped
- 6 garlic cloves, minced
- ½ teaspoon dried thyme
- 4 cups low-sodium beef broth
- 1 cup water
- ½ cup pearl barley

1. Season the meat with the salt and pepper.
2. In an Instant Pot, heat the oil over high heat. Add the meat and brown on all sides. Remove the meat from the pot and set aside.
3. Add the mushrooms to the pot and cook for 1 to 2 minutes, until they begin to soften. Remove the mushrooms and set aside with the meat.
4. Add the onion, carrots, and celery to the pot. Sauté for 3 to 4 minutes until the vegetables begin to soften. Add the garlic and continue to cook until fragrant, about 30 seconds longer.
5. Return the meat and mushrooms to the pot, then add the thyme, beef broth, and water. Set the pressure to high and cook for 15 minutes. Let the pressure release naturally.
6. Open the Instant Pot and add the barley. Use the slow cooker function on the Instant Pot, affix the lid (vent open), and continue to cook for 1 hour until the barley is cooked through and tender. Serve.

PER SERVING
Calories: 245 | Total Fat: 9g | Protein: 21g | Carbohydrates: 19g | Fiber: 4g | Sugar: 3g | Sodium: 516mg

Roasted Carrot Leek Soup
Prep time: 4 minutes | Cook time: 30 minutes | Serves 3-4

- 6 carrots, cut into thirds
- 1 cup chopped onion
- 1 fennel bulb, cubed
- 2 garlic cloves, crushed
- 2 tablespoons avocado oil
- 1 teaspoon sea salt
- 1 teaspoon black pepper
- 2 cups almond milk

1. At 400 degrees F, preheat your oven. Line a baking sheet with parchment paper.
2. Add the carrots, onion, fennel, garlic, and avocado oil, and toss to coat.
3. Season the veggies with black pepper and salt, and toss again.
4. Transfer the vegetables to the prepared baking sheet, and roast for almost 30 minutes. Remove from the oven and allow the vegetables to cool.
5. In a high-speed blender, blend together the almond milk and roasted vegetables until creamy and smooth. Adjust the seasonings, if necessary, and add additional milk if you prefer a thinner consistency.
6. Pour into 2 large or 4 suitable bowls and enjoy.

PER SERVING
Calories: 55 | Total Carbohydrates: 12g | Net Carbohydrates: 2g | Protein: 1.8g | Fat: 2g | Suger: 1g | Fiber: 2g

Red Lentil Soup
Prep time: 10 minutes | Cook time: 55 minutes | Serves 8

- 1 teaspoon extra-virgin olive oil
- 1 sweet onion, chopped
- 1 tablespoon minced garlic
- 4 celery stalks, with the greens, chopped
- 3 carrots, peeled and diced
- 3 cups red lentils, picked over, washed, and drained
- 4 cups low-sodium vegetable broth
- 3 cups water
- 2 bay leaves
- 2 teaspoons chopped fresh thyme
- Sea salt
- Freshly ground black pepper

1. Place a large stockpot on medium-high heat and add the oil.
2. Sauté the onion and garlic until translucent, about 3 minutes.
3. Stir in the celery and carrots and sauté 5 minutes.
4. Add the lentils, broth, water, and bay leaves, and bring the soup to a boil.
5. Reduce the heat to low and simmer until the lentils are soft and the soup is thick, about 45 minutes.
6. Remove the bay leaves and stir in the thyme.
7. Season with salt and pepper and serve.

PER SERVING
Calories: 284 | Total Fat: 2g | Cholesterol: 0mg | Sodium: 419mg | Total Carbohydrates: 47g | Sugar: 4g | Fiber: 24g | Protein: 20g

Lamb Vegetable Stew

Prep time: 15 minutes | Cook time: 35 minutes | Serves 2

- 1 lb. diced lamb shoulder
- 1 lb. chopped winter vegetables
- 1 cup vegetable broth
- 1 tablespoon yeast extract
- 1 tablespoon star anise spice mix

1. Mix all the recipe ingredients in your instant pot.
2. Cook on stew for 35 minutes.
3. Release the pressure naturally.

PER SERVING

Calories: 320 | Total Carbohydrates: 10g | Net Carbohydrates: 1.2g | Protein: 42g | Fat: 8g | Suger: 1g | Fiber: 2g

Thai Peanut and Shrimp Soup with Carrots

Prep time: 10 minutes | Cook time: 15 minutes | Serves 4

- 1 tablespoon coconut oil
- 1 tablespoon Thai red curry paste
- 3 garlic cloves, minced
- ½ onion, sliced
- 2 cups carrots, chopped
- ½ cup whole unsalted peanuts
- 4 cups low-sodium chicken broth
- ½ cup unsweetened almond milk
- ½ pound (227 g) shrimp, peeled and deveined
- Minced fresh cilantro, for garnish
- An immersion blender

1. Melt the coconut oil in a large skillet over medium-high heat until shimmering.
2. Add the red curry paste and cook for 1 minutes, stirring continuously.
3. Add the garlic, onion, carrots, and peanuts to the skillet, and sauté for 2 to 3 minutes until the garlic is fragrant.
4. Pour in the chicken broth and whisk to combine, then bring to a boil.
5. Reduce the heat to low and allow to simmer until the carrots are tender when pierced with a fork, about 5 to 6 minutes.
6. Purée the soup with an immersion blender until smooth.
7. Add the almond milk and mix well. Stir in the shrimp and cook for an additional 3 minutes , or until the flesh is totally pink and opaque.
8. Remove from the heat and ladle the soup into four bowls. Sprinkle the cilantro on top for garnish before serving.

PER SERVING

Calories: 240 | Fat: 14.3g | Protein: 14.2g | Carbohydrates: 17.3g | Fiber: 5.2g | Sugar: 6.2g | Sodium: 618mg

Tomato and Kale Soup

Prep time: 10 minutes | Cook time: 15 minutes | Serves 4

- 1 tablespoon extra-virgin olive oil
- 1 medium onion, chopped
- 2 carrots, finely chopped
- 3 garlic cloves, minced
- 4 cups low-sodium vegetable broth
- 1 (28-ounce) can crushed tomatoes
- ½ teaspoon dried oregano
- ¼ teaspoon dried basil
- 4 cups chopped baby kale leaves
- ¼ teaspoon salt

1. In a large pot, heat the oil over medium heat. Add the onion and carrots to the pan. Sauté for 3 to 5 minutes until they begin to soften. Add the garlic and sauté for 30 seconds more, until fragrant.
2. Add the vegetable broth, tomatoes, oregano, and basil to the pot and bring to a boil. Reduce the heat to low and simmer for 5 minutes.
3. Using an immersion blender, purée the soup.
4. Add the kale and simmer for 3 more minutes. Season with the salt. Serve immediately.

PER SERVING

Calories: 170 | Total Fat: 5g | Protein: 6g | Carbohydrates: 31g | Fiber: 9g | Sugar: 13g | Sodium: 600mg

Irish Lamb Stew

Prep time: 15 minutes | Cook time: 35 minutes | Serves 2

- 1.5 lb. diced lamb shoulder
- 1lb chopped vegetables
- 1 cup beef broth
- 3 minced onions
- 1 tablespoon ghee

1. Mix all the recipe ingredients in your instant pot.
2. Cook on stew for 35 minutes.
3. Release the pressure naturally.

PER SERVING

Calories: 330 | Total Carbohydrates: 9g | Net Carbohydrates: 2g | Protein: 49g | Fat: 12g | Suger: 1g | Fiber: 2g

Classic Gazpacho
Prep time: 15 minutes | Cook time: 0 minutes | Serves 4

- 3 pounds (1.4 kg) ripe tomatoes, chopped
- 1 cup low-sodium tomato juice
- ½ red onion, chopped
- 1 cucumber, peeled, seeded, and chopped
- 1 red bell pepper, seeded and chopped
- 2 celery stalks, chopped
- 2 tablespoons chopped fresh parsley
- 2 garlic cloves, chopped
- 2 tablespoons extra-virgin olive oil
- 2 tablespoons red wine vinegar
- 1 teaspoon honey
- ½ teaspoon salt
- ¼ teaspoon freshly ground black pepper

1. In a blender jar, combine the tomatoes, tomato juice, onion, cucumber, bell pepper, celery, parsley, garlic, olive oil, vinegar, honey, salt, and pepper. Pulse until blended but still slightly chunky.
2. Adjust the seasonings as needed and serve.
3. To store, transfer to a nonreactive, airtight container and refrigerate for up to 3 days.

PER SERVING
Calories: 172 | Fat: 8.1g | Protein: 5.1g | Carbohydrates: 23.9g | Fiber: 6.1g | Sugar: 16g | Sodium: 333mg

Gazpacho
Prep time: 15 minutes | Serves 4

- 3 pounds ripe tomatoes, chopped
- 1 cup low-sodium tomato juice
- ½ red onion, chopped
- 1 cucumber, peeled, seeded, and chopped
- 1 red bell pepper, seeded and chopped
- 2 celery stalks, chopped
- 2 tablespoons chopped fresh parsley
- 2 garlic cloves, chopped
- 2 tablespoons extra-virgin olive oil
- 2 tablespoons red wine vinegar
- 1 teaspoon honey
- ½ teaspoon salt
- ¼ teaspoon freshly ground black pepper

1. In a blender jar, combine the tomatoes, tomato juice, onion, cucumber, bell pepper, celery, parsley, garlic, olive oil, vinegar, honey, salt, and pepper. Pulse until blended but still slightly chunky.
2. Adjust the seasonings as needed and serve.
3. To store, transfer to a nonreactive, airtight container and refrigerate for up to 3 days.

PER SERVING
Calories: 170 | Total Fat: 8g | Protein: 5g | Carbohydrates: 24g | Fiber: 6g | Sugar: 16g | Sodium: 332mg

Avocado and Goat Cheese Toast
Prep time: 5 minutes | Serves 2

- 2 slices whole-wheat thin-sliced bread
- ½ avocado
- 2 tablespoons crumbled goat cheese
- Salt

1. In a toaster or broiler, toast the bread until browned.
2. Remove the flesh from the avocado. In a medium bowl, use a fork to mash the avocado flesh. Spread it onto the toast.
3. Sprinkle with the goat cheese and season lightly with salt.
4. Add any toppings and serve.

PER SERVING
Calories: 137 | Total Fat: 6g | Protein: 5g | Carbohydrates: 18g | Fiber: 5g | Sugar: 0g | Sodium: 195mg

Harvest Salad
Prep time: 15 minutes | Cook time: 25 minutes | Serves 6

- 10 oz. kale, deboned and chopped
- 1 ½ cup blackberries
- ½ butternut squash, cubed
- ¼ cup goat cheese, crumbled
- Maple Mustard Salad Dressing
- 1 cup raw pecans
- 1/3 cup raw pumpkin seeds
- ¼ cup dried cranberries
- 3 1/2 tbsp. olive oil
- 1 ½ tbsp. sugar free maple syrup
- 3/8 tsp salt, divided
- Pepper, to taste
- Nonstick cooking spray

1. Heat oven to 400 degrees. Spray a baking sheet with cooking spray.
2. Spread squash on the prepared pan, add 1 ½ tablespoons oil, 1/8 teaspoon salt, and pepper to squash and stir to coat the squash evenly. Bake 20-25 minutes.
3. Place kale in a large bowl. Add 2 tablespoons oil and ½ teaspoon salt and massage it into the kale with your hands for 3-4 minutes.
4. Spray a clean baking sheet with cooking spray. In a medium bowl, stir together pecans, pumpkin seeds, and maple syrup until nuts are coated. Pour onto prepared pan and bake 8-10 minutes, these can be baked at the same time as the squash.
5. To assemble the salad: place all of the Ingredients in a large bowl. Pour dressing over and toss to coat. Serve.

PER SERVING
Calories: 436 | Total Carbohydrates: 24g | Net Carbohydrates: 17g | Protein: 9g | Fat: 37g | Suger: 5g | Fiber: 7g

Chopped Vegetable-Barley Salad

Prep time: 25 minutes | Cook time: 25 minutes | Serves 4

- 1 cup water
- ½ cup pearl barley
- 4 cups chopped Brussels sprouts
- 3 celery stalks, chopped
- 2 carrots, chopped
- 2 cups chopped cauliflower
- 1 cup halved cherry tomatoes
- 1 scallion, both white and green parts, chopped
- ¼ cup extra-virgin olive oil
- Juice of 1 lemon
- Sea salt
- Freshly ground black pepper

1. In a small saucepan, combine the water and barley and bring to a boil over medium-high heat. Cover, reduce the heat to low, and simmer for 22 to 25 minutes, until tender but with a bit of bite.
2. While the barley is cooking, in a large bowl, toss together the Brussels sprouts, celery, carrots, bell pepper, cauliflower, tomatoes, pumpkin seeds, and scallion until well mixed.
3. In a small bowl, whisk the oil and lemon juice and season with salt and pepper.
4. Add the cooked barley and dressing to the salad, toss to combine, and serve.

PER SERVING

Calories: 339 | Total Fat: 18g | Saturated Fat: 3g | Sodium: 115mg | Carbohydrates: 40g | Sugar: 5g | Fiber: 11g | Protein: 10g

Cauliflower Leek Soup

Prep time: 10 minutes | Cook time: 20 minutes | Serves 2

- Avocado oil cooking spray
- 2½ cups chopped leeks (2 to 3 leeks)
- 2½ cups cauliflower florets
- ⅓ cup low-sodium vegetable broth
- ½ cup half-and-half
- ¼ teaspoon salt
- ¼ teaspoon freshly ground black pepper

1. Heat a large stockpot over medium-low heat. When hot, coat the cooking surface with cooking spray. Put the leeks and cauliflower into the pot.
2. Increase the heat to medium and cover the pan. Cook for 10 minutes, stirring halfway through.
3. Add the garlic and cook for 5 minutes.
4. Add the broth and deglaze the pan, stirring to scrape up the browned bits from the bottom.
5. Transfer the broth and vegetables to a food processor or blender and add the half-and-half, salt, and pepper. Blend well.

PER SERVING

Calories: 173 | Total Fat: 7g | Protein: 6g | Carbohydrates: 24g | Fiber: 5g | Sugar: 8g | Sodium: 487mg

Roasted Tomato Bell Pepper Soup

Prep time: 20 minutes | Cook time: 35 minutes | Serves 6

- 2 tablespoons extra-virgin olive oil, plus more to oil the pan
- 16 plum tomatoes, cored, halved
- 4 red bell peppers, seeded, halved
- 4 celery stalks, coarsely chopped
- 1 sweet onion, cut into eighths
- 4 garlic cloves, lightly crushed
- Sea salt
- 6 cups low-sodium chicken broth
- 2 tablespoons chopped fresh basil
- 2 ounces goat cheese

1. Preheat the oven to 400°F.
2. Lightly oil a large baking dish with olive oil.
3. Place the tomatoes cut-side down in the dish, then scatter the bell peppers, celery, onion, and garlic on the tomatoes.
4. Drizzle the vegetables with 2 tablespoons of olive oil and lightly season with salt and pepper.
5. Roast the vegetables until they are soft and slightly charred, about 30 minutes.
6. Remove the vegetables from the oven and purée them in batches, with the chicken broth, in a food processor or blender until smooth.
7. Transfer the puréed soup to a medium saucepan over medium-high heat and bring the soup to a simmer.
8. Stir in the basil and goat cheese just before serving.

PER SERVING

Calories: 188 | Total Fat: 10g | Cholesterol: 10mg | Sodium: 826mg | Total Carbohydrates: 21g | Sugar: 14g | Fiber: 6g | Protein: 8g

Kale Cobb Salad

Prep time: 25 minutes | Serves 2

- 6 cups torn baby kale, thoroughly washed and dried
- ½ cup store-bought balsamic dressing or Everyday Balsamic Vinaigrette
- 3 celery stalks, sliced
- 2 hard-boiled eggs, chopped
- 1 apple, cored and chopped
- ¼ red onion, chopped
- ¼ cup crumbled low-fat blue cheese
- ¼ cup chopped pecans

1. In a large bowl, toss together the kale and dressing. Let stand for 10 minutes.
2. Evenly divide the kale among 4 plates.
3. Top each salad with equal amounts of celery, chicken, eggs, apple, onion, blue cheese, and pecans. Serve immediately.

PER SERVING

Calories: 373 | Total Fat: 16g | Saturated Fat: 6g | Sodium: 532mg | Carbohydrates: 34g | Sugar: 16g | Fiber: 6g | Protein: 32g

Chapter 11
Snacks and Desserts

Apple Pie Parfait

Prep time: 25 minutes | Serves 2

- 1 apple, peeled, cored, and chopped
- 1 teaspoon maple syrup (optional)
- ½ teaspoon ground cinnamon
- 1 cup low-fat vanilla yogurt, divided
- ¼ cup chopped almonds or pecans, divided
- ¼ cup whipped coconut cream (see tip)

1. In a small bowl, toss together the apple, maple syrup (if using), and cinnamon until well mixed.
2. Layer ¼ cup yogurt in the bottom of a tall, wide glass or small bowl. Then layer in ¼ of the apple and 1 tablespoon almonds. Repeat the layering and top the glass with 2 tablespoons of whipped coconut cream.
3. Repeat with a second glass or bowl and serve immediately.

PER SERVING

Calories: 311 | Total Fat: 20g | Saturated Fat: 11g | Sodium: 87mg | Carbohydrates: 23g | Sugar: 15g | Fiber: 4g | Protein: 9g

Roasted Squash with Thyme

Prep time: 10 minutes | Cook time: 20 minutes | Serves 4

- 1 (1½-pound) delicata squash
- 1 tablespoon olive oil
- ½ teaspoon dried thyme
- ¼ teaspoon salt
- ¼ teaspoon black pepper

1. At 400 degrees F, preheat your oven. Line the baking sheet with parchment paper and set aside for later use.
2. Add the squash strips, olive oil, thyme, salt, and pepper in a suitable bowl, and then toss to coat the squash strips well.
3. Place the squash strips on the prepared baking sheet in a single layer. Roast for almost 20 minutes, flipping the strips halfway through. Remove from the oven and serve on plates.

PER SERVING

Calories: 80 | Total Carbohydrates: 6.2g | Net Carbohydrates: 1.2g | Protein: 7g | Fat: 13g | Suger: 2g | Fiber: 3.3g

Grilled Sesame Tofu

Prep time: 45 minutes | Cook time: 10 minutes | Serves 6

- 1½ tablespoons brown rice vinegar
- 1 scallion
- 1 tablespoon ginger root
- 1 tablespoon no-sugar-added applesauce
- 2 tablespoons naturally brewed soy sauce
- ¼ teaspoon dried red pepper flakes
- 2 teaspoons sesame oil, toasted
- 1 (14-ounce / 397-g) package extra-firm tofu
- 2 tablespoons cilantro
- 1 teaspoon sesame seeds

1. Combine the vinegar, scallion, ginger, applesauce, soy sauce, red pepper flakes, and sesame oil in a suitable bowl. Stir to mix well.
2. Dunk the tofu pieces in the bowl, then refrigerate to marinate for almost 30 minutes.
3. Preheat a grill pan over medium-high heat. Place the tofu on the grill pan with tongs, reserve the marinade, then grill for 8 minutes, flipping halfway through.
4. Transfer the tofu to a large plate and sprinkle with cilantro leaves and sesame seeds. Serve with the marinade alongside.

PER SERVING

Calories: 189 | Total Carbohydrates: 7.9g | Net Carbohydrates: 4.5g | Protein: 6g | Fat: 10g | Suger: 1g | Fiber: 5g

Parmesan Crisps

Prep time: 5 minutes | Cook time: 5 minutes | Serves 2

- 1 cup grated Parmesan cheese

1. Preheat the oven to 400°F (205°C). Line a rimmed baking sheet with parchment paper.
2. Spread the Parmesan on the prepared baking sheet into 4 mounds, spreading each mound out so it is flat but not touching the others.
3. Bake until brown and crisp, 3 to 5 minutes.
4. Cool for 5 minutes. Use a spatula to remove to a plate to continue cooling.

PER SERVING

Calories: 216 | Fat: 14.1g | Protein: 19.1g | Carbohydrates: 2g | Fiber: 0g | Sugar: 1.5g | Sodium: 765mg

Jewel Yams with Nutmeg

Prep time: 7 minutes | Cook time: 45 minutes | Serves 8

- 2 medium jewel yams
- 2 tablespoons unsalted butter
- Juice of 1 large orange
- 1½ teaspoons ground cinnamon
- ¼ teaspoon ground ginger
- ¾ teaspoon ground nutmeg
- ⅛ teaspoon ground cloves

1. Set the oven at 355 degrees F. Arrange the yam dices on a rimmed baking sheet in a single layer. Set aside.
2. Add the butter, orange juice, cinnamon, ginger, nutmeg, and garlic cloves to a medium saucepan over medium-low heat. Cook for 3 to 5 minutes, stirring occasionally. Spoon the sauce over the yams and toss to coat well.
3. Bake in the preheated oven for 40 minutes. Let the yams cool for 8 minutes on the baking sheet before removing and serving.

PER SERVING
Calories: 129 | Total Carbohydrates: 10g | Net Carbohydrates: 6g | Protein: 11g | Fat: 9g | Suger: 1g | Fiber: 3g

Grilled Peach and Coconut Yogurt Bowls

Prep time: 5 minutes | Cook time: 10 minutes | Serves 4

- 2 peaches, halved and pitted
- ½ cup plain nonfat Greek yogurt
- 1 teaspoon pure vanilla extract
- ¼ cup unsweetened dried coconut flakes
- 2 tablespoons unsalted pistachios, shelled and broken into pieces

1. Preheat the broiler to high. Arrange the rack in the closest position to the broiler.
2. In a shallow pan, arrange the peach halves, cut-side up. Broil for 6 to 8 minutes until browned, tender, and hot.
3. In a small bowl, mix the yogurt and vanilla.
4. Spoon the yogurt into the cavity of each peach half.
5. Sprinkle 1 tablespoon of coconut flakes and 1½ teaspoons of pistachios over each peach half. Serve warm.

PER SERVING
Calories: 102 | Total Fat: 5g | Protein: 5g | Carbohydrates: 11g | Fiber: 2g | Sugar: 8g | Sodium: 12mg

Tomato Mozzarella Skewers

Prep time: 5 minutes | Cook time: 5 minutes | Serves 2

- 12 cherry tomatoes
- 8 (1-inch) pieces reduced-fat mozzarella cheese
- 12 basil leaves
- ¼ cup Italian vinaigrette, for serving

1. Thread the tomatoes, cheese and bay leave alternatively through the skewers.
2. Place the Caprese skewers on a large plate and baste with the Italian vinaigrette. Serve immediately.

PER SERVING
Calories: 116 | Total Carbohydrates: 4g | Net Carbohydrates: 3g | Protein: 12g | Fat: 12g | Suger: 0.5g | Fiber: 6g

Ice Cream with Warm Strawberry Rhubarb Sauce

Prep time: 10 minutes | Cook time: 15 minutes | Serves 4

- 1 cup sliced strawberries
- 1 cup chopped rhubarb
- 2 tablespoons water
- 1 tablespoon honey
- ½ teaspoon cinnamon
- 4 (¼-cup) scoops sugar-free vanilla ice cream

1. In a medium pot, combine the strawberries, rhubarb, water, honey, and cinnamon. Bring to a simmer on medium heat, stirring. Reduce the heat to medium-low. Simmer, stirring frequently, until the rhubarb is soft, about 15 minutes. Allow to cool slightly.
2. Place 1 scoop of ice cream into each of 4 bowls. Spoon the sauce over the ice cream.

PER SERVING
Calories: 86 | Total Fat: 2g | Saturated Fat: 1g | Sodium: 37mg | Carbohydrates: 16g | Fiber: 3g | Protein: 3g

Raspberry Pumpkin Muffin

Cook time: 1 hour | Serves 1

- 1 cup Canned pumpkin puree
- ½ cup Coconut flour
- ¾ cup Almond flour (blanched)
- ½ cup Stevia
- 3 tablespoons Tapioca
- 1 tablespoon Baking powder
- 1 tablespoon Cinnamon
- a pinch Nutmeg
- ¼ teaspoon Salt
- 4 large (whites and yolks separated) Eggs
- ½ cup Coconut oil
- 1½ teaspoons Vanilla extract
- 1½ cups Frozen raspberries
- 10 drops Liquid stevia

1. Start by preheating the oven to 350°F.
2. Prepare the muffin tin by placing muffin paper cups in all the molds.
3. Take a large mixing bowl and add in the almond flour, coconut flour, tapioca starch, stevia, cinnamon, baking powder, sea salt, and nutmeg. Mix well.
4. Now add in the pumpkin puree, egg yolks, coconut oil, vanilla extract, and stevia drops. Whisk until the flour mixture and wet ingredients are well-incorporated. The muffin batter is ready
5. Take another large bowl and add in the egg whites. Beat the eggs until you see stiff peaks being formed.
6. Transfer the frozen raspberries and beaten egg whites to the muffin batter. Use a spatula to gently fold the berries and egg whites into the batter.
7. Use a deep spoon to scoop out the batter and pour it into the lined muffin molds. Make sure you fill the muffin paper cups to the top.
8. Transfer the muffin tin to the preheated oven and bake for about 25 minutes. Insert a toothpick into the center to check if it comes out clean; if so, the muffins are perfectly baked.
9. Once done, take the muffin tin out of the oven and let the muffins cool for about 5 minutes.
10. Remove the muffins from the tin and let them cool until they reach room temperature.
11. Serve and enjoy!

PER SERVING

Fat: 31.9g | Protein: 4.8g | Carbohydrates: 11.2g

Easy Cauliflower Hush Puppies

Prep time: 15 minutes | Cook time: 10 minutes | Serves 16

- 1 whole cauliflower, including stalks and florets, roughly chopped
- ¾ cup buttermilk
- ¾ cup low-fat milk
- 1 medium onion, chopped
- 2 medium eggs
- 2 cups yellow cornmeal
- 1½ teaspoons baking powder
- ½ teaspoon salt

1. In a blender, combine the cauliflower, buttermilk, milk, and onion and purée. Transfer to a large mixing bowl.
2. Crack the eggs into the purée, and gently fold until mixed.
3. In a medium bowl, whisk the cornmeal, baking powder, and salt together.
4. Gently add the dry ingredients to the wet ingredients and mix until just combined, taking care not to overmix.
5. Working in batches, place ⅓-cup portions of the batter into the basket of an air fryer.
6. Set the air fryer to 390°F (199°C), close, and cook for 10 minutes. Transfer the hush puppies to a plate. Repeat until no batter remains.
7. Serve warm with greens.

PER SERVING

Calories: 180 | Fat: 8.1g | Protein: 4.1g | Carbohydrates: 27.9g | Fiber: 6.1g | Sugar: 11g | Sodium: 251mg

Garlicky Kale Chips

Prep time: 5 minutes | Cook time: 15 minutes | Serves 1

- ¼ teaspoon garlic powder
- Pinch cayenne to taste
- 1 tablespoon olive oil
- ½ teaspoon sea salt, or to taste
- 1 (8-ounce) bunch kale

1. At 355 degrees F, preheat your oven. Line 2 baking sheets with parchment paper.
2. Toss the garlic powder, cayenne pepper, olive oil, and salt in a suitable bowl, then dunk the kale in the bowl. Situate kale in a single layer on 1 of the baking sheets.
3. Arrange the sheet in the preheated oven and bake for 7 minutes. Remove the sheet from the oven and pour the kale into the single layer of the other baking sheet.
4. Move the sheet of kale back to the oven and bake for another 7 minutes. Serve and enjoy.

PER SERVING

Calories: 116 | Total Carbohydrates: 4g | Net Carbohydrates: 3g | Protein: 12g | Fat: 12g | Suger: 0.5g | Fiber: 6g

Banana and Carrot Flax Muffins

Prep time: 20 minutes | Cook time: 40 minutes | Serves 8

- ¼ teaspoon cloves
- ¼ cup tapioca starch
- ½ cup stevia
- 1 teaspoon salt
- 1 teaspoon nutmeg
- 1 tablespoon cinnamon
- 1 teaspoon baking soda
- 1 teaspoon baking powder
- 1¾ cups almond flour
- 4 tablespoons flax meal
- 1½ cups water
- 1 teaspoon vanilla extract
- ⅓ cup coconut oil
- 1 medium banana, mashed
- 1½ cups carrots, shredded

1. Preheat the oven to 350°F (180°C). Line an 8-cup muffin tin with paper cups.
2. Soak the flax meal in water in a bowl for 5 minutes to make the flax egg.
3. Combine all the dry ingredients in a large bowl. Stir to mix well.
4. Make a well in the dry mixture, then pour the flax egg, vanilla extract, and coconut oil in the well. Stir to mix well, then mix in the banana and carrots.
5. Divide the mixture among 8 muffins cups, then bake in the preheated oven for 40 minutes or until the top springs back when you press the muffins with your fingers.
6. Remove the muffins from the oven and allow to cool before serving.

PER SERVING

Calories: 135 | Fat: 9.5g | Protein: 1.5g | Carbohydrates: 14g | Fiber: 1.6g | Sugar: 4.2g | Sodium: 464mg

Berry Smoothie Pops

Prep time: 5 minutes | Cook time: 30 minutes | Serves 6

- 2 cups frozen mixed berries
- ½ cup unsweetened plain almond milk
- 1 cup plain nonfat Greek yogurt
- 2 tablespoons hemp seeds

1. Place all the ingredients in a blender and process until finely blended.
2. Pour into 6 clean ice pop molds and insert sticks.
3. Freeze for 3 to 4 hours until firm.

PER SERVING

Calories: 70 | Total Fat: 2g | Protein: 5g | Carbohydrates: 9g | Fiber: 3g | Sugar: 2g | Sodium: 28mg

Cauliflower Mash

Prep time: 7 minutes | Cook time: 20 minutes | Serves 4

- 1 head cauliflower, cored and cut into large florets
- ½ teaspoon kosher salt
- ½ teaspoon garlic pepper
- 2 tablespoons plain Greek yogurt
- ¾ cup freshly grated Parmesan cheese
- 1 tablespoon unsalted butter or ghee (optional)
- Chopped fresh chives

1. Pour 1 cup of water into the electric pressure cooker and insert a steamer basket or wire rack.
2. Place the cauliflower in the basket.
3. Close and lock the lid of the pressure cooker. Set the valve to sealing.
4. Cook on high pressure for 5 minutes.
5. When the cooking is complete, hit Cancel and quick release the pressure.
6. Once the pin drops, unlock and remove the lid.
7. Remove the cauliflower from the pot and pour out the water. Return the cauliflower to the pot and add the salt, garlic pepper, yogurt, and cheese. Use an immersion blender or potato masher to purée or mash the cauliflower in the pot.
8. Spoon into a serving bowl, and garnish with butter (if using) and chives.

PER SERVING

Calories: 141 | Fat: 6.1g | Protein: 12.1g | Carbohydrates: 11.9g | Fiber: 4.1g | Sugar: 5g | Sodium: 591mg

Apple Crunch

Prep time: 13 minutes | Cook time: 11 minutes | Serves 4

- 3 apples, peeled, cored, and sliced (about 1½ pounds)
- 1 teaspoon pure maple syrup
- 1 teaspoon apple pie spice or ground cinnamon
- ¼ cup unsweetened apple juice, apple cider, or water
- ¼ cup low-sugar granola

1. In the electric pressure cooker, combine the apples, maple syrup, apple pie spice, and apple juice.
2. Close and lock the lid of the pressure cooker. Set the valve to sealing.
3. Cook on high pressure for 2 minutes.
4. When the cooking is complete, hit Cancel and quick release the pressure.
5. Once the pin drops, unlock and remove the lid.
6. Spoon the apples into 4 serving bowls and sprinkle each with 1 tablespoon of granola.

PER SERVING

Calories: 103 | Total Fat: 1g | Protein: 1g | Carbohydrates: 26g | Fiber: 4g | Sugar: 18g | Sodium: 13mg

Appendix 1 Measurement Conversion Chart

Volume Equivalents (Dry)	
US STANDARD	METRIC (APPROXIMATE)
1/8 teaspoon	0.5 mL
1/4 teaspoon	1 mL
1/2 teaspoon	2 mL
3/4 teaspoon	4 mL
1 teaspoon	5 mL
1 tablespoon	15 mL
1/4 cup	59 mL
1/2 cup	118 mL
3/4 cup	177 mL
1 cup	235 mL
2 cups	475 mL
3 cups	700 mL
4 cups	1 L

Volume Equivalents (Liquid)		
US STANDARD	US STANDARD (OUNCES)	METRIC (APPROXIMATE)
2 tablespoons	1 fl.oz.	30 mL
1/4 cup	2 fl.oz.	60 mL
1/2 cup	4 fl.oz.	120 mL
1 cup	8 fl.oz.	240 mL
1 1/2 cup	12 fl.oz.	355 mL
2 cups or 1 pint	16 fl.oz.	475 mL
4 cups or 1 quart	32 fl.oz.	1 L
1 gallon	128 fl.oz.	4 L

Temperatures Equivalents	
FAHRENHEIT(F)	CELSIUS(C) APPROXIMATE)
225 °F	107 °C
250 °F	120 ° °C
275 °F	135 °C
300 °F	150 °C
325 °F	160 °C
350 °F	180 °C
375 °F	190 °C
400 °F	205 °C
425 °F	220 °C
450 °F	235 °C
475 °F	245 °C
500 °F	260 °C

Weight Equivalents	
US STANDARD	METRIC (APPROXIMATE)
1 ounce	28 g
2 ounces	57 g
5 ounces	142 g
10 ounces	284 g
15 ounces	425 g
16 ounces (1 pound)	455 g
1.5 pounds	680 g
2 pounds	907 g

Appendix 2 The Dirty Dozen and Clean Fifteen

The Environmental Working Group (EWG) is a nonprofit, nonpartisan organization dedicated to protecting human health and the environment Its mission is to empower people to live healthier lives in a healthier environment. This organization publishes an annual list of the twelve kinds of produce, in sequence, that have the highest amount of pesticide residue-the Dirty Dozen-as well as a list of the fifteen kinds of produce that have the least amount of pesticide residue-the Clean Fifteen.

THE DIRTY DOZEN	
The 2016 Dirty Dozen includes the following produce. These are considered among the year's most important produce to buy organic:	
Strawberries	Spinach
Apples	Tomatoes
Nectarines	Bell peppers
Peaches	Cherry tomatoes
Celery	Cucumbers
Grapes	Kale/collard greens
Cherries	Hot peppers
The Dirty Dozen list contains two additional itemskale/collard greens and hot peppers-because they tend to contain trace levels of highly hazardous pesticides.	

THE CLEAN FIFTEEN	
The least critical to buy organically are the Clean Fifteen list. The following are on the 2016 list:	
Avocados	Papayas
Corn	Kiw
Pineapples	Eggplant
Cabbage	Honeydew
Sweet peas	Grapefruit
Onions	Cantaloupe
Asparagus	Cauliflower
Mangos	
Some of the sweet corn sold in the United States are made from genetically engineered (GE) seedstock. Buy organic varieties of these crops to avoid GE produce.	

Appendix 3 Index

A

all-purpose flour 50, 53
allspice 15
almond 5, 14
ancho chile 10
ancho chile powder 5
apple 9
apple cider vinegar 9
arugula 51
avocado 11

B

bacon 52
balsamic vinegar 7, 12, 52
basil 5, 8, 11, 13
beet 52
bell pepper 50, 51, 53
black beans 50, 51
broccoli 51, 52, 53
buns 52
butter 50

C

canola oil 50, 51, 52
carrot 52, 53
cauliflower 5, 52
cayenne 5, 52
cayenne pepper 52
Cheddar cheese 52
chicken 6
chili powder 50, 51
chipanle pepper 50
chives 5, 6, 52
cinnamon 15
coconut 6
Colby Jack cheese 51
coriander 52
corn 50, 51
corn kernels 50
cumin 5, 10, 15, 50, 51, 52

D

diced panatoes 50
Dijon mustard 7, 12, 13, 51
dry onion powder 52

E

egg 14, 50, 53
enchilada sauce 51

F

fennel seed 53
flour 50, 53
fresh chives 5, 6, 52
fresh cilantro 52
fresh cilantro leaves 52
fresh dill 5
fresh parsley 6, 52
fresh parsley leaves 52

G

garlic 5, 9, 10, 11, 13, 14, 50, 51, 52, 53
garlic powder 8, 9, 52, 53

H

half-and-half 50
hemp seeds 8
honey 9, 51

I

instant rice 51

K

kale 14
kale leaves 14
ketchup 53
kosher salt 5, 10, 15

L

lemon 5, 6, 14, 51, 53
lemon juice 6, 8, 11, 13, 14, 51
lime 9, 12
lime juice 9, 12
lime zest 9, 12

M

maple syrup 7, 12, 53
Marinara Sauce 5
micro greens 52
milk 5, 50
mixed berries 12
Mozzarella 50, 53
Mozzarella cheese 50, 53
mushroom 51, 52
mustard 51, 53
mustard powder 53

N

nutritional yeast 5

O

olive oil 5, 12, 13, 14, 50, 51, 52, 53
onion 5, 50, 51
onion powder 8
oregano 5, 8, 10, 50

P

panatoes 50, 52
paprika 5, 15, 52
Parmesan cheese 51, 53
parsley 6, 52
pesto 52
pink Himalayan salt 5, 7, 8, 11
pizza dough 50, 53
pizza sauce 50
plain coconut yogurt 6
plain Greek yogurt 5
porcini powder 53
potato 53

R

Ranch dressing 52
raw honey 9, 12, 13
red pepper flakes 5, 8, 14, 15, 51, 53
ricotta cheese 53

S

saffron 52
Serrano pepper 53
sugar 10
summer squash 51

T

tahini 5, 8, 9, 11
thyme 50
toasted almonds 14
tomato 5, 50, 52, 53
turmeric 15

U

unsalted butter 50
unsweetened almond milk 5

V

vegetable broth 50
vegetable stock 51

W

white wine 8, 11
wine vinegar 8, 10, 11

Y

yogurt 5, 6

Z

zucchini 50, 51, 52, 53

DOROTHY G. EBERLY

Printed in Great Britain
by Amazon